SharePoint D 2007: Basic

Student Manual

INSTRUCTOR: CHRIS ALEXANDER
E-MAIL: CALEXANDER@NHNASHVILLE.COM

Australia • Canada • Mexico • Singapore
Spain • United Kingdom • United States

SharePoint Designer 2007: Basic

VP and GM, Training Group:	Michael Springer
Series Product Managers:	Charles G. Blum and Adam A. Wilcox
Writer:	Dave Fink
Developmental Editor:	Brandon Heffernan
Copyeditor:	Cathy Albano
Keytester:	Cliff Coryea
Series Designer:	Adam A. Wilcox
Cover Designer:	Abby Scholz

COPYRIGHT © 2007 Course Technology, a division of Thomson Learning. Thomson Learning is a trademark used herein under license.

ALL RIGHTS RESERVED. No part of this work may be reproduced, transcribed, or used in any form or by any means—graphic, electronic, or mechanical, including photocopying, recording, taping, Web distribution, or information storage and retrieval systems—without the prior written permission of the publisher.

For more information contact:

Course Technology
25 Thomson Place
Boston, MA 02210

Or find us on the Web at: www.course.com

For permission to use material from this text or product, submit a request online at: www.thomsonrights.com

Any additional questions about permissions can be submitted by e-mail to: thomsonrights@thomson.com

Trademarks
Course ILT is a trademark of Course Technology.

Some of the product names and company names used in this book have been used for identification purposes only and may be trademarks or registered trademarks of their respective manufacturers and sellers.

Disclaimer
Course Technology reserves the right to revise this publication and make changes from time to time in its content without notice.

Student Manual
ISBN 10: 1-4239-5113-1
ISBN 13: 978-1-4239-5113-1

Student Manual with data CD
ISBN 10: 1-4239-5115-8
ISBN 13: 978-1-4239-5115-5

Printed in the United States of America

1 2 3 4 5 6 7 8 9 GLOB 09 08 07

Contents

Introduction iii
    Topic A: About the manual iv
    Topic B: Setting your expectations vii
    Topic C: Re-keying the course xi

Getting started 1-1
    Topic A: Internet basics 1-2
    Topic B: The SharePoint Designer workspace 1-4
    Topic C: Page editing 1-12
    Topic D: HTML 1-20
    Unit summary: Getting started 1-24

Web sites 2-1
    Topic A: Site planning basics 2-2
    Topic B: Creating a Web site 2-4
    Topic C: Templates 2-10
    Unit summary: Web sites 2-20

Text formatting 3-1
    Topic A: Text basics 3-2
    Topic B: Structural formatting 3-11
    Topic C: Cascading Style Sheets 3-16
    Unit summary: Text formatting 3-28

Web page layout 4-1
    Topic A: Basic CSS layout 4-2
    Topic B: Basic layout techniques 4-10
    Unit summary: Web page layout 4-23

Images 5-1
    Topic A: Image formats and properties 5-2
    Topic B: Working with images 5-10
    Unit summary: Images 5-16

Hyperlinks 6-1
    Topic A: Basic hyperlinks 6-2
    Topic B: Link styles 6-14
    Topic C: Image maps 6-18
    Unit summary: Hyperlinks 6-21

Tables 7-1
    Topic A: Working with tables 7-2
    Topic B: Table-based layouts 7-16
    Unit summary: Tables 7-20

Publishing 8-1
    Topic A: Proofing tools 8-2
    Topic B: Web site publishing 8-6

Unit summary: Publishing 8-13

Course summary　　　　　　　　　　　　　　　　　　　　　　S-1
Topic A: Course summary S-2
Topic B: Continued learning after class S-3

Quick reference　　　　　　　　　　　　　　　　　　　　　　Q-1

Glossary　　　　　　　　　　　　　　　　　　　　　　　　　G-1

Index　　　　　　　　　　　　　　　　　　　　　　　　　　I-1

Introduction

After reading this introduction, you'll know how to:

A Use Course Technology ILT manuals in general.

B Use prerequisites, a target student description, course objectives, and a skills inventory to set your expectations properly for the course.

C Re-key this course after class.

Topic A: About the manual

Course Technology ILT philosophy

Course Technology ILT manuals facilitate your learning by providing structured interaction with the software itself. While we provide text to explain difficult concepts, the hands-on activities are the focus of our courses. By paying close attention as your instructor leads you through these activities, you'll learn the skills and concepts effectively.

We believe strongly in the instructor-led class. During class, focus on your instructor. Our manuals are designed and written to facilitate your interaction with your instructor, and not to call attention to manuals themselves.

We believe in the basic approach of setting expectations, delivering instruction, and providing summary and review afterwards. For this reason, lessons begin with objectives and end with summaries. We also provide overall course objectives and a course summary to provide both an introduction to and closure on the entire course.

Manual components

The manuals contain these major components:

- Table of contents
- Introduction
- Units
- Course summary
- Quick reference
- Glossary
- Index

Each element is described below.

Table of contents

The table of contents acts as a learning roadmap.

Introduction

The introduction contains information about our training philosophy and our manual components, features, and conventions. It contains target student, prerequisite, objective, and setup information for the specific course.

Units

Units are the largest structural component of the course content. A unit begins with a title page that lists objectives for each major subdivision, or topic, within the unit. Within each topic, conceptual and explanatory information alternates with hands-on activities. Units conclude with a summary comprising one paragraph for each topic, and an independent practice activity that gives you an opportunity to practice the skills you've learned.

The conceptual information takes the form of text paragraphs, exhibits, lists, and tables. The activities are structured in two columns, one telling you what to do, the other providing explanations, descriptions, and graphics.

Course summary

This section provides a text summary of the entire course. It's useful for providing closure at the end of the course. The course summary also indicates the next course in this series, if there is one, and lists additional resources you might find useful as you continue to learn about the software.

Quick reference

The quick reference is an at-a-glance job aid summarizing some of the more common features of the software.

Glossary

The glossary provides definitions for all of the key terms used in this course.

Index

The index at the end of this manual makes it easy for you to find information about a particular software component, feature, or concept.

Manual conventions

We've tried to keep the number of elements and the types of formatting to a minimum in the manuals. This aids in clarity and makes the manuals more classically elegant looking. But there are some conventions and icons you should know about.

Item	Description
Italic text	In conceptual text, indicates a new term or feature.
Bold text	In unit summaries, indicates a key term or concept. In an independent practice activity, indicates an explicit item that you select, choose, or type.
`Code font`	Indicates code or syntax.
`Longer strings of ▶ code will look ▶ like this.`	In the hands-on activities, any code that's too long to fit on a single line is divided into segments by one or more continuation characters (▶). This code should be entered as a continuous string of text.
Select **bold item**	In the left column of hands-on activities, bold sans-serif text indicates an explicit item that you select, choose, or type.
Keycaps like ⏎ ENTER	Indicate a key on the keyboard you must press.

Hands-on activities

The hands-on activities are the most important parts of our manuals. They're divided into two primary columns. The "Here's how" column gives short instructions to you about what to do. The "Here's why" column provides explanations, graphics, and clarifications. Here's a sample:

Do it!

A-1: Creating a commission formula

Here's how	Here's why
1 Open Sales	This is an oversimplified sales compensation worksheet. It shows sales totals, commissions, and incentives for five sales reps.
2 Observe the contents of cell F4	F4 ▼ = =E4*C_Rate The commission rate formulas use the name "C_Rate" instead of a value for the commission rate.

For these activities, we have provided a collection of data files designed to help you learn each skill in a real-world business context. As you work through the activities, you modify and update these files. Of course, you might make a mistake and therefore want to re-key the activity starting from scratch. To make it easy to start over, you rename each data file at the end of the first activity in which the file is modified. Our convention for renaming files is to add the word "My" to the beginning of the file name. In the above activity, for example, a file called "Sales" is being used for the first time. At the end of this activity, you would save the file as "My sales," thus leaving the "Sales" file unchanged. If you make a mistake, you can start over using the original "Sales" file.

In some activities, however, it might not be practical to rename the data file. If you want to retry one of these activities, ask your instructor for a fresh copy of the original data file.

Topic B: Setting your expectations

Properly setting your expectations is essential to your success. This topic will help you do that by providing:

- Prerequisites for this course
- A description of the target student
- A list of the objectives for the course
- A skills assessment for the course

Course prerequisites

Before taking this course, you should be familiar with personal computers and the use of a keyboard and a mouse. Furthermore, this course assumes that you've completed the following courses or have equivalent experience:

- *Windows 2000: Basic* or *Windows XP: Basic*
- *Internet Explorer 6.0: Basic*

Target student

The target students for this course should be familiar with personal computers, having worked with Microsoft Windows 2000 or later, and Internet Explorer 6.0. You'll get the most out of this course if your goal is to become proficient at building Web sites quickly.

Course objectives

These overall course objectives will give you an idea about what to expect from the course. It's also possible that they'll help you see that this course isn't the right one for you. If you think you either lack the prerequisite knowledge or already know most of the subject matter to be covered, you should let your instructor know that you think you are misplaced in the class.

After completing this course, you'll know how to:

- Discuss basic Internet and Web concepts, identify components of the SharePoint Designer interface, make basic adjustments to Web pages, and select elements.

- Plan the design and structure of a site, create a new one-page site and add folders and pages to it, create and edit a template, and apply a template to existing pages.

- Import content into a page from an external document, convert line breaks to paragraph breaks, insert non-breaking spaces and symbols, apply structural tags, create lists, create an external style sheet, and establish element and class styles.

- Define content sections; create and apply ID styles; apply margins, padding, and borders to an element; create a two-column layout; and clear an element to prevent it from wrapping around a floated section.

- Discuss image file formats, adjust basic image properties, apply alternate text to an image, and arrange images relative to adjacent content.

- Create links, link bars, e-mail links, and bookmarks, customize link styles, create image maps, and link hotspots to bookmarks.

- Insert and format tables and table cells, insert and format rows and columns, create table captions, and work with nested tables in a table-based layout.

- Check for spelling errors and broken hyperlinks throughout a site, identify options associated with publishing sites, and connect to a server by using FTP.

Skills inventory

Use the following form to gauge your skill level entering the class. For each skill listed, rate your familiarity from 1 to 5, with 5 being the most familiar. *This isn't a test*. Rather, it's intended to provide you with an idea of where you're starting from at the beginning of class. If you're wholly unfamiliar with all the skills, you might not be ready for the class. If you think you already understand all of the skills, you might need to move on to the next course in the series. In either case, you should let your instructor know as soon as possible.

Skill	1	2	3	4	5
Identifying interface components					
Switching site views					
Inserting and editing page content					
Previewing a page in a browser					
Viewing HTML					
Selecting page elements					
Planning a site					
Creating a one-page Web site					
Creating new pages and folders					
Creating a template					
Defining editable regions in a template					
Setting page properties					
Applying a template to site pages					
Importing content from an external file					
Converting line breaks to paragraph breaks					
Inserting symbols and non-breaking spaces					
Creating headings					
Creating lists					
Creating and attaching a style sheet					
Defining and applying element styles and class styles					
Defining content sections by using <div> tags					
Creating and applying ID styles					

Skill	1	2	3	4	5
Creating fixed and fluid layouts					
Creating a two-column layout					
Applying margins, padding, and borders					
Specifying alternate text for images					
Formatting and arranging images on a page					
Creating hyperlinks					
Creating and modifying link bars					
Creating bookmark links					
Creating and editing image maps					
Applying CSS link styles					
Inserting tables					
Formatting table and cell properties					
Inserting rows and columns					
Creating table captions					
Working with nested tables					
Checking for spelling errors in a site					
Checking for broken links in a site					
Connecting to a server by using secure FTP					

Topic C: Re-keying the course

If you have the proper hardware and software, you can re-key this course after class. This section explains what you need in order to do so and how to do it.

Hardware requirements

Your personal computer should have:

- A keyboard and a mouse
- A Pentium 700 MHz processor (or higher)
- At least 512 MB RAM (1 GB recommended)
- 2 GB of available hard drive space
- A CD-ROM drive
- An SVGA or higher resolution monitor, at 1024 × 768

Software requirements

You also need the following software:

- Microsoft Windows XP Service Pack (SP) 2 or later or Microsoft Windows Server 2003 (or later)
- Microsoft SharePoint Designer 2007
- Microsoft Outlook Express or another e-mail client (required to complete activity A-3 in the unit titled "Hyperlinks")

Network requirements

The following network components and connectivity are also required for re-keying this course:

- Internet access, for the following purposes:
  - Downloading the latest critical updates and service packs from www.windowsupdate.com
  - Downloading the student data files from www.courseilt.com (if necessary)

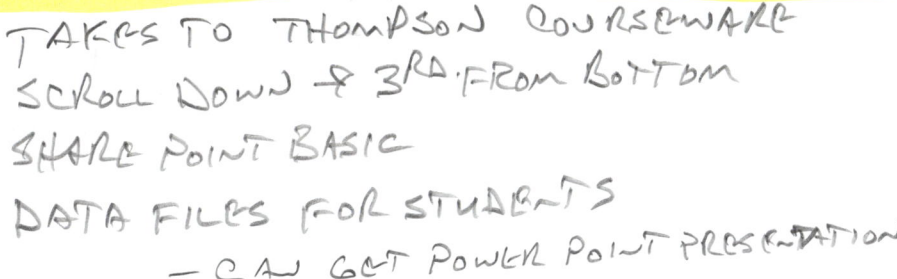

Setup instructions to re-key the course

Before you re-key the course, you need to perform the following steps.

1. Install Windows XP Professional on an NTFS partition according to the software manufacturer's instructions.
2. Install Microsoft SharePoint Designer 2007 according to the software manufacturer's instructions.
3. If necessary, reset any defaults that you've changed. If you don't wish to reset the defaults, you can still re-key the course, but some activities might not work exactly as documented.
4. Adjust the computer's display settings as follows:
    a. Right-click the desktop and choose Properties to open the Display Properties dialog box.
    b. On the Settings tab, change the Color quality to 16 bit or higher and the Screen resolution to 1024 by 768 pixels. (If your monitor is small, consider using a higher screen resolution, if possible.)
    c. On the Appearance tab, set Windows and buttons to Windows XP style.
    d. Click OK. If you're prompted to accept the new settings, click OK and click Yes. Then, if necessary, close the Display Properties dialog box.
5. Adjust Internet properties as follows:
    a. Start Internet Explorer. Choose Tools, Internet Options.
    b. On the General tab, click Use Blank, and click Apply.
    c. On the Advanced tab, under Security, check Allow active content to run in files on My Computer, and click Apply. (This option appears only if you updated Windows XP with Service Pack 2.)
    d. On the Connections tab, click Setup to start the Internet Connection Wizard.
    e. Click Cancel. A message box appears.
    f. Check "Do not show the Internet Connection wizard in the future," and click Yes.
    g. Close the Internet Options dialog box, and close Internet Explorer.
6. Display file extensions.
    a. Start Windows Explorer.
    b. Choose Tools, Folder Options and select the View tab.
    c. Clear the check box for Hide extensions for known file types.
    d. Close Windows Explorer.
7. Create a folder called Student Data at the root of the hard drive (C:\).
8. Download the student data files for the course.
    a. Connect to www.courseilt.com/ilt_downloads.cfm.
    b. Click the link for Microsoft SharePoint Designer to display a page of course listings, and then click the link for SharePoint Designer 2007: Basic.
    c. Click the link for downloading the student data files, and follow the instructions that appear on your screen.
9. Copy the data files to the Student Data folder.

CertBlaster software

CertBlaster pre- and post-assessment software is available for this course. To download and install this free software, complete the following steps:

1. Go to www.courseilt.com/certblaster.
2. Click the link for SharePoint Designer 2007.
3. Save the .EXE file to a folder on your hard drive. (Note: If you skip this step, the CertBlaster software will not install correctly.)
4. Click Start and choose Run.
5. Click Browse and then navigate to the folder that contains the .EXE file.
6. Select the .EXE file and click Open.
7. Click OK and follow the on-screen instructions. When prompted for the password, enter **c_spd07**.

Unit 1
Getting started

Unit time: 50 minutes

Complete this unit, and you'll know how to:

A Discuss basic Internet and HTML concepts.

B Identify components of the SharePoint Designer interface.

C Identify basic page elements, insert text and images, and preview a page in a browser.

D Select page elements by using the Quick Tag Selector.

Topic A: Internet basics

Explanation

Before you get started with SharePoint Designer to design and create Web sites, you should have a basic understanding of the Internet, the Web, and HTML.

The Internet and the Web

The *Internet* is a vast network of electronic networks that belong to universities, businesses, organizations, governments, and individuals all over the world. The World Wide Web, or simply *Web*, is one of many services of the Internet. Other Internet services include e-mail, File Transfer Protocol (FTP), and instant messaging.

To view Web pages and other content, you need a Web browser, such as Internet Explorer, Netscape, Safari, or Firefox. Web content typically includes text, images, and multimedia files. Each page or resource has a unique address known as a *Uniform Resource Locater (URL)*.

A *Web site* is a collection of linked pages. The top-level page is commonly referred to as the *home page*. Home pages are often named index.htm, because most Web servers are configured to look for that file name as the Web site's root, or top-level file. A home page typically provides hyperlinks to navigate to other pages within the site or to external pages. A *hyperlink*, or *link* for short, is text or an image that, when clicked, connects the user to another page or Web site.

HTML

Hypertext Markup Language, or *HTML*, is a standard markup language on the Web. You use HTML to construct and present your Web site's content. An *HTML document* is a plain text file that contains HTML code. Exhibit 1-1 shows an example of a simple HTML document. You create HTML documents automatically when you use SharePoint Designer to generate pages. However, you can also hand-code HTML documents by using any text editor, such as Notepad (Windows) or TextEdit (Macintosh). HTML documents have either an .htm or .html file extension.

HTML code contains your text content and defines the basic structure of a Web page. It can contain links and references to images, multimedia files, and many elements. When a browser opens a Web page, the text typically loads quickly, while images and embedded media files might take longer.

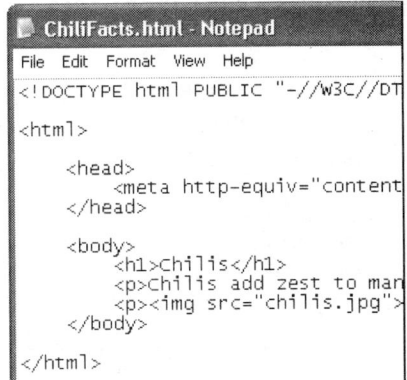 

Exhibit 1-1: A simple Web page shown as HTML and in a browser

Do it!

A-1: Discussing the Web and HTML

Questions and answers

1 What's the difference between the Internet and the World Wide Web?

2 What other Internet services are there?

3 What's a Web page?

4 What's a Web site?

5 What's a Web browser?

6 What is HTML?

Topic B: The SharePoint Designer workspace

Explanation

SharePoint Designer 2007 is Web authoring software that helps you design and create Web pages and Web sites. When you make changes to a page in the SharePoint Designer workspace, SharePoint Designer automatically generates the required code for you. You can also write or edit the code yourself.

To begin creating Web pages with SharePoint Designer, choose Start, All Programs, Microsoft Office, Microsoft Office SharePoint Designer 2007. By default, SharePoint Designer displays a blank, untitled HTML document. To open an existing document, choose File, Open, and navigate to the location of the document you want to open.

Interface elements

Exhibit 1-2 shows SharePoint Designer's default interface components, which include toolbars, task panes, the Views bar, and the status bar.

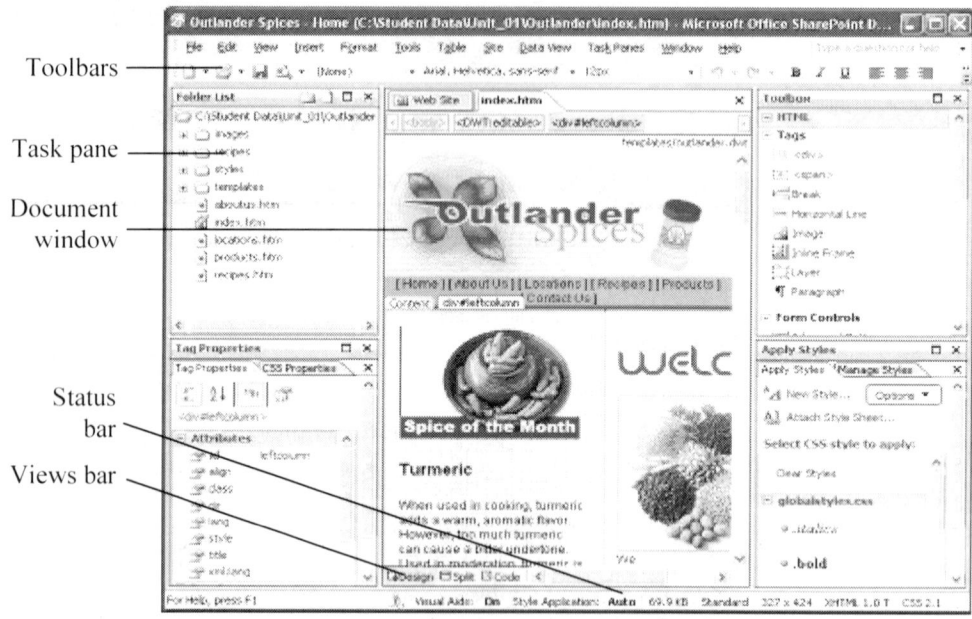

Exhibit 1-2: The SharePoint Designer interface

The following table describes these components.

Component	Description
Toolbars	Provide buttons for fast and easy access to various commands.
Task panes	There are several task panes that surround the document window. These task panes include the Folder List pane, the Tag Properties pane, and the Apply Styles pane. They provide options to perform common tasks. For example, you can use task panes to create new pages and folders or apply CSS styles.
Status bar	Displays information about open documents and certain application options. For example, the status bar shows download statistics for a page and includes a pop-up window to change the page size.
Views bar	Allows you to change the view of an open document quickly, or for all the pages in a site. When a page is open, you can select Design view, Code View, or Split View (both Design and Code views). You can also preview pages. When no documents are open, you can change how you view the overall site. You can switch between Hyperlinks, Folders, and Navigation views, as well as views for controlling Remote Site information, Reports, and Tasks.
Document window	Displays open Web pages. When no pages in a site are open, the document window shows a hierarchical view of the contents of the site folder.

Task panes

When you launch SharePoint Designer for the first time, four task panes are visible—two on each side of the document window. The panes expand and collapse, so you can view them as needed, or hide them when you're ready to move on to another task. You can also open other task panes by selecting them from the Task Panes menu. The following table briefly describes the four default task panes.

Task Pane	Description
Folder List	Provides a hierarchical list of documents and folders in the site. When you don't have any documents open, the same hierarchical list is visible in the larger pane in the center of the work area.
Toolbox	Provides a list of shortcuts for various types of Web page functions, such as inserting commonly used HTML tags and form controls.
Manage Styles/ Apply Styles	Provides a way to manage and apply CSS styles. The task pane title changes, based on the active tab. For example, if you activate the Apply Styles tab, the title bar changes to represent the Apply Styles pane.
Tag Properties/ CSS Properties	Provides a way to apply specific properties to HTML tags and to CSS styles without having to work within the page code. Similar to the Manage Styles pane, the task pane title changes based on the active tab.

1–6 SharePoint Designer 2007: Basic

Do it!

B-1: Identifying interface components

Here's how	Here's why
1 Choose **Start**, **All Programs**, **Microsoft Office**, **Microsoft Office SharePoint Designer 2007**	To start SharePoint Designer 2007. A blank HTML document appears.
2 In the upper-right corner of the document window, click as shown	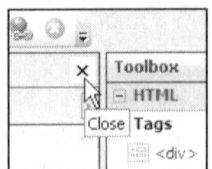 To close the blank document (untitled_1.htm).
3 Choose **File**, **Open…**	The Open File dialog box appears.
4 Navigate to the current unit folder	
5 Open the Outlander folder	The Outlander folder contains documents and subfolders that comprise the site.
Select **index.htm** and click **Open**	To open the Outlander Spices home page. The page appears in the Document window.
6 Locate the Folder List pane	All the folders and documents included in the site are listed in this pane. When you open a page from a site that was created by using SharePoint Designer, the site contents are also displayed.
7 Locate the Toolbox pane	The Toolbox pane contains a list of shortcuts for commonly used Web page elements.
8 Locate the Apply Styles pane	The Apply Styles pane includes two tabs: Apply Styles and Manage Styles. The Manage Styles tab shows a list of CSS styles used throughout the site.
9 In the status bar, point as shown	 (At the bottom of the application window.) To view the download statistics for the page. A pop-up appears with information about the page, including the file size and number of links in the page.

Arranging task panes

Explanation

Although the default task panes are docked on either side of the document window, you can customize the interface by shifting them to other locations or by floating them (undocking them so they can be positioned anywhere on the screen).

- To hide or display a task pane, choose Task Panes and the name of the task pane.
- To expand or collapse a task pane, click the Maximize/Minimize button in the upper-right corner of the task pane title bar.
- To float a task pane, drag the title bar of the task pane away from the other docked task panes, as shown in Exhibit 1-3. To dock a floating task pane, double-click the title bar.
- To reset all task panes to their default positions, choose Task Panes, Reset Workspace Layout.

Exhibit 1-3: Dragging a task pane title bar to float the task pane

Do it! **B-2: Exploring task panes**

Here's how	Here's why
1 Locate the Tag Properties pane	On the left side of the application window.
In the upper-right corner, click as shown	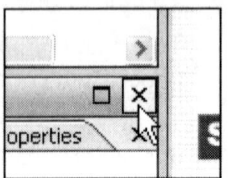
	To close this task pane. The Folder List pane expands to fill the left column.
2 In the Apply Styles pane, click the Manage Styles tab, as shown	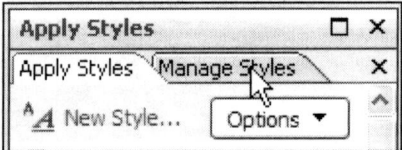
	To activate the Manage Styles pane. Notice that the pane's name has changed to reflect the active tab.
In the Manage Styles pane, click as shown	
	The Manage Styles pane expands to fill the entire right column, and you can clearly see the entire list of CSS styles applied to the document. The Toolbox pane is still open, but collapsed.
Click the Minimize icon, as shown	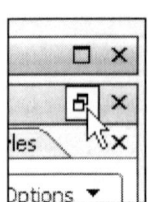
	To return the Manage Styles pane to its default size.

3	Point to the Manage Styles pane title bar, as shown	
		The pointer changes to indicate that you can drag the pane to a desired location.
	Drag to the left until it docks below the document window	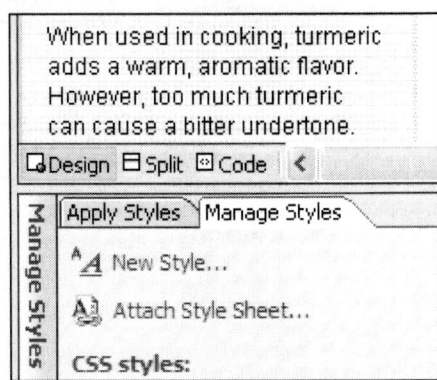
		You might want to dock some of the task panes into this position, or you might prefer to use floating task panes.
4	Point to the Manage Styles pane title bar and drag upward	(The title bar now runs vertically on the left side of the pane.) To convert it to a floating task pane. You can move this pane anywhere on screen—even outside the boundaries of the application window. Depending on your development preferences and the size of your monitor, you might choose to arrange certain panes this way.
5	Point to the bottom edge of the Manage Styles pane	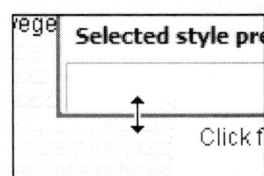
		The pointer changes to indicate that you can resize the pane vertically.
	Drag the bottom edge down	To view more of the contents of the pane.
6	Choose **Task Panes**, **Reset Workspace Layout**	To return all panes to their default locations.

Site views

Explanation

When no documents are open, the Document window displays the contents of the site folder (similar to the Folder List pane). Also, the Views bar shows six site-related view choices. The following table briefly describes each view.

Item	Description
Folders (default)	Shows the files and folders of the Web site. The root folder is shown by default. Double-click a subfolder to view its contents, or double-click a document to open it. To revert back to the root folder, click the Up One Level button in the top-right corner of the window, or click the root folder icon in the Folder List pane.
Remote Web Site	If you've established any remote Web site settings, they're visible in this view. To establish remote settings, click the Remote Web Site Properties button at the top of the window. You can establish properties for Sharepoint Services, WebDAV, or FTP, all of which are explained more fully later in the course.
Reports	Provides a range of reports for the site, such as the number of images used, the number of internal or external hyperlinks that exist, or even the number of style sheet and template links that exist.
Navigation	Shows a graphical representation of the navigation structure of a Web site. The home page is the starting point, and any linked pages are listed below it.
Hyperlinks	Shows all the hyperlinks in a Web site at a single glance. The home page is shown by default, but you can view the links for other pages by selecting them in the Folder List pane. You can view other links associated with linked pages by clicking the small plus or minus signs.
Tasks	If you've created any tasks for a site, they're visible in this view. This feature works best when a site is being created or maintained by more than one person, as it helps maintain consistency. Tasks, such as creating a good navigation structure or editing a design mockup, can be assigned to the site in order of importance.

Do it!

B-3: Switching site views

Here's how	Here's why
1 At the top of the document window, click as shown 	To switch from the home page to the default site view. The contents of the Web site are listed in the document window.
In the list of site contents, select **index.htm**	
2 In the Views bar, click [Reports]	The window shows a site summary of reports, including the number of images used and hyperlinks that exist.
3 Click [Navigation]	(In the Views bar.) The window shows a graphical representation of the navigational structure of the site.
4 Click [Hyperlinks]	The window shows links associated with the home page (index.htm).
5 In the Folder List pane, click aboutus.htm	(To select it.) The links associated with the About Us page appear in the window.
Click as shown	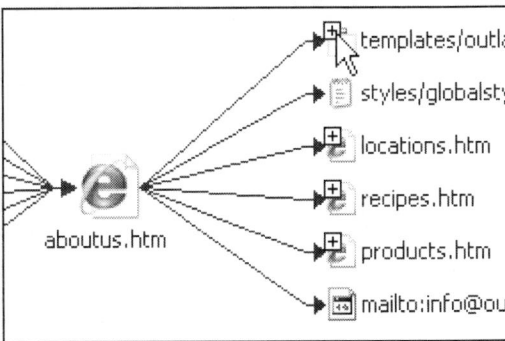
	To view the links associated with the template document.
Collapse template/outlander.dwt	Click the minus sign next to templates/outlander.dwt.
6 Right-click anywhere in the pane and choose **Hyperlinks to Pictures**	To view images linked to the document.
7 In the Views bar, click 	To return to the list of site contents.

Topic C: Page editing

Explanation

Editing content in SharePoint Designer is a lot like using a word processor. You can add, edit, delete, and rearrange content, such as text, tables, and images. You can save a group of Web pages as a site; much in the same way you can save word processor pages together as a single document.

Pages in a word processor document are typically designed to be read in sequence—when you finish reading page six, for example, you continue on to page seven. However, pages in a Web site can be linked in any order, or they can follow no order at all.

Web page elements

Web pages can include many types of content, including text, images, and links, as illustrated in Exhibit 1-4.

Exhibit 1-4: A sample Web page

The following table describes some typical Web page elements.

Element	Description
Text	Words, phrases, sentences, headings, and paragraphs.
Images	Graphic files, typically in the .gif, .jpg, or .png format.
Links	Text or images that connect a browser to another location when clicked. The destination might be another Web page, a different area of the current page, or some other resource.
Image map	A single graphic that includes multiple links.
Forms	Interactive pages consisting of text input fields, check boxes, and buttons that allow the user to submit data to a server for processing and data storage.
Tables	Grid structures consisting of rows and columns meant primarily to contain tabular data such as a product list with associated prices. Tables can also help you control the layout and spacing of elements on a page. However, a site is generally easier to maintain if you use CSS to control page layout.

Do it!

C-1: Discussing Web page elements

Questions and answers

1 What's the difference between an image and an image map?

2 What are links?

3 What's a table used for?

4 What are forms?

Explanation

Basic content

To add basic content such as text or images to a Web page, you can simply click a page to place the insertion point and either type the text you want or import an image. With Web pages, it's important to understand that text and images are always in line with each other. For example, if you place an image before a paragraph of text, the image remains at the beginning of the paragraph, even if you add more text before the image. The new text pushes the image further down the page, unlike page layout applications in which the text might flow around the image.

Inserting content

To add text to a page, you can type at the insertion point, or you can copy or paste text from another document. To add images to a page, you can drag an image from the Folder List pane to the location where you want the image on the page. When you drag an image, a small arrow appears next to the pointer, as shown in the first example in Exhibit 1-5. This is a visual indicator that you're adding an image to the page.

When you drag an image from the Folder List task pane, the pointer shows a small arrow.

The image pushes the following text further down the page.

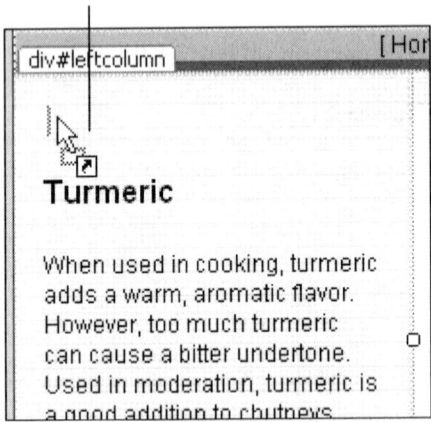 

Exhibit 1-5: Adding an image to a page by dragging from the Folder List pane

You can also add images by placing the insertion point on the page where you want the image and clicking the Insert Picture from File button in the Common toolbar. Using this method, you need to navigate to the location of the image.

Common, Standard, and Formatting toolbars

As you add content to pages, you'll often use the options in the Common toolbar, the default set of tools that appear at the top of the SharePoint Designer window. The Common toolbar is comprised of the most commonly used options from the Standard toolbar, shown in Exhibit 1-6, and the Formatting toolbar, shown in Exhibit 1-7. For some editing tasks, you might wish to use the Standard and Formatting toolbars instead of the Common toolbar. The following tables describe some of the commonly used buttons and lists from these toolbars.

Exhibit 1-6: The Standard toolbar

Button	Name
	New Document
	Open
	Save
	Preview in Microsoft Internet Explorer
	Insert Picture From File
	Insert Hyperlink
	Refresh
	Show Formatting Marks

Exhibit 1-7: The Formatting toolbar

Button/List	Name
(None)	Style
Arial, Helvetica, sans-serif	Font
12px	Font Size
B	Bold
I	Italic
U	Underline

Do it!

C-2: Inserting and editing basic content

Here's how	Here's why
1 At the top of the Document window, activate index.htm	To switch from the site view to the home page.
2 In the paragraph below the Welcome heading, click between the words "providing" and "spices"	grocery and specialty stores a you can order directly from this dedicated to providing spices and variety. Discover a whole look for an Outlander Spices k you!
	To position the insertion point before the word "spices." You'll modify the text in this section.
3 Type **the finest**	To add new text to the existing paragraph. (Be sure to add a space at the end.) This type of text editing is no different from working in a word processor.
4 In the Monthly Recipes text, select **Outlander Chicken**	ustomers. This month we are recipe for Outlander Chicken pes...
5 In the Common toolbar, click **B**	To make the text bold. Next, you'll add an image to the page.
6 Place the insertion point at the end of the last paragraph	the adding spices to t of allspice and your an alternative.
Press ← ENTER	To add a new paragraph after the text.

7 In the Folder List pane, expand
   the images subfolder

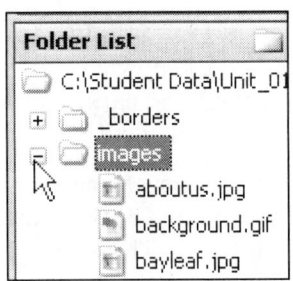

   Scroll down the list to locate
   spices_graphic.gif

   Drag spices_graphic.gif from the
   task pane to the new paragraph

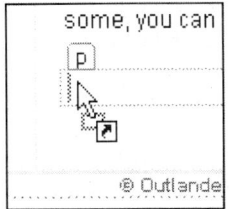

                                    To add the image to the page.

   Click **OK**   To close the Accessibility Properties dialog box.

8 Click another area of the page   To deselect the image and view the results.

9 In the Common toolbar, click   To save the document.

Previewing Web pages

Explanation

You can preview a Web page while you're working on it so that you can see how it will appear in a particular Web browser. You can do this directly in SharePoint Designer or by opening the page you're working on in a browser.

To preview a page in SharePoint Designer, click the Preview button in the View bar at the bottom of the document window. When you do, the page is displayed as it would appear in a browser. The size of the document window determines the width of the preview page. So if you're working on a smaller monitor and have task panes open on either side of the document, the content on the page might appear very narrow and out of alignment. You need to take this into consideration when you preview pages within SharePoint Designer.

Preview options

Generally, it's good practice to preview your pages directly in multiple browsers, because your site visitors view your site by using a wide variety of browsers and versions. Not all browsers render pages the same way—there are often minor differences in how each browser interprets HTML and CSS code, and these differences can affect the way a page looks and functions.

To preview a page in a browser, select a browser and window size from the Preview list in the Standard toolbar, or press F12 to preview the page quickly in Microsoft Internet Explorer. SharePoint Designer is configured to use Microsoft Internet Explorer as the main browser within which you can preview pages. If you have a different browser defined as the default browser on your machine, you can opt to use that browser as well. You can even preview a page in multiple browsers, as shown in the options in Exhibit 1-8. Each option also provides a way to preview a page by using a specific browser window size.

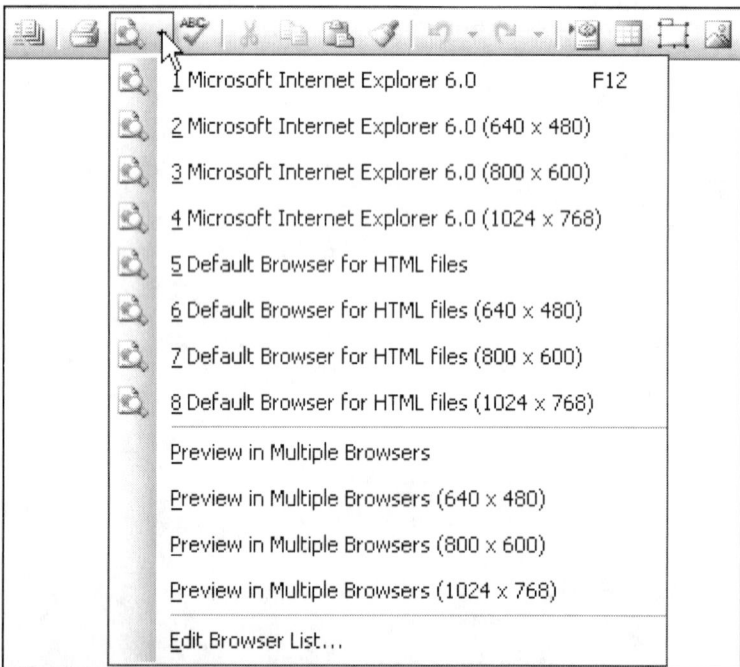

Exhibit 1-8: The Preview list in the Standard toolbar

Do it!

C-3: Previewing a page

Here's how	Here's why
1 In the Common toolbar, click	SharePoint Designer shows the page as it would appear in Internet Explorer. The center content looks very narrow, pushing the text into a narrower column. SharePoint Designer sets the preview page width according to the amount of screen space available between the task panes. The page would expand more if you were to close some of the task panes.
2 In the Common toolbar, click as shown	
	A list of options for previewing pages appears.
3 From the list, choose **Windows Internet Explorer 7.0 (800x600)**	Internet Explorer launches, and the page displays. The size of the browser window is automatically set to 800 × 600, which is a size that fits most monitor widths.
4 Close the browser	To return to SharePoint Designer.

Topic D: HTML

Explanation

HTML, or Hypertext Markup Language, consists of *tags* that define the structure of elements in a Web page. A *tag* is a pre-defined marker that tells the Web browser how to interpret or display the content it contains. HTML tags are enclosed in angular brackets (< >). Most HTML tags consist of a beginning tag and an accompanying ending tag. The ending tag includes a forward slash (/), which tells the browser that the tag instruction has ended. For example, the following code is a snippet of text that uses the <strong> tag to define bold text:

```
Outlander Spices makes the <strong>best</strong> seasonings.
```

A Web browser would display this text as follows:

Outlander Spices makes the **best** seasonings.

Document structure

The standard tags that begin every HTML document are <html>, <head>, and <body>. The <html> element is considered the *root element,* or top-level element. It defines the document as an HTML document. All other HTML tags are nested within it. An HTML document is then divided into two sections, the head section and the body section.

The <head> section contains the <title> element, which defines the document's title, as well as style sheet information, meta information, scripts, and other code or resources that aren't rendered on the page.

The <body> section contains all the content (text, HTML code, images, and so on) that's rendered on a page. If you can see it in a browser, the code for it is in the body section.

Exhibit 1-9 shows the basic structure of an HTML document. Notice that some tags are inside other tags, and there's an ending tag for each starting tag.

```
 1  <!DOCTYPE html PUBLIC "-//W3C//DTD XHTM
 2  <html xmlns="http://www.w3.org/1999/xht
 3
 4  <head>
 5  <meta http-equiv="Content-Language" con
 6  <meta http-equiv="Content-Type" content
 7  <title>Outlander Spices - Home</title>
 8  <meta name="Microsoft Border" content="
 9  </head>
10
11  <body style="margin: 0; background-imag
12  <div id="leftcolumn">
13  <img src="images/spice_of_month.gif" st
14  <h2>Turmeric</h2>
15  <p>When used in cooking, turmeric adds
16  too much turmeric can cause a bitter un
17  </p>
18  </div>
19  </body>
20
21  </html>
```

Lines 4–9: Head section
Lines 11–19: Body section

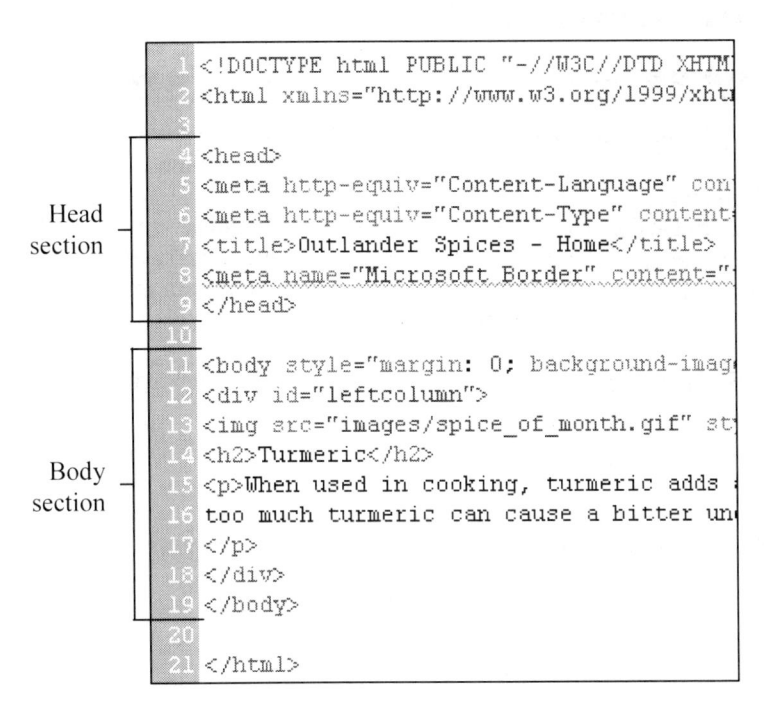

Exhibit 1-9: Basic HTML document structure

IntelliSense

Most of the editing you do in SharePoint Designer doesn't require you to work directly in Code view. However, a good understanding of HTML is beneficial for fixing problems that arise as you work or for removing excess code when you insert and remove page elements. Some designers prefer to hand-code certain aspects of a page.

If you choose to hand-code a portion of a page, the IntelliSense feature in SharePoint Designer makes the process more efficient, because it automatically helps prevent all kinds of common errors, including incorrect tag usage. IntelliSense includes statement completion and displays the parameters available for the code you're writing. It also provides typing aids to speed up the code writing process.

For example, if you're writing code to insert a table, when you type the letter t, IntelliSense displays a menu in which the table tag appears selected. Pressing Enter replaces the t with the required table tags. Then, pressing Spacebar opens a menu containing attributes, such as border and align, that are available for the table tag. Code IntelliSense is available for HTML, CSS (cascading style sheets), XSL (Extensible Stylesheet Language), JScript, VBScript, JavaScript, and ASP.NET.

The Code View toolbar

You can also use the Code View toolbar, as shown in Exhibit 1-10, to make hand-coding more efficient. The toolbar contains several typing aids that automate tasks, such as inserting comments, applying word wrap, inserting bookmarks, and finding matching tags.

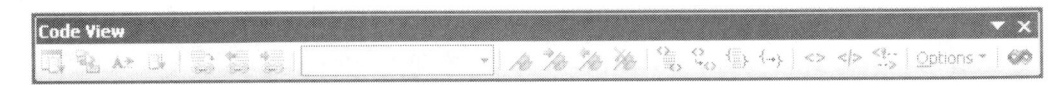

Exhibit 1-10: The Code View toolbar

Do it!

D-1: Viewing HTML

Here's how	Here's why
1 In the Views bar, click [Split]	To split the document window into Code view and Design view
2 In Design view, click an image on the page	(To select it.) Code view scrolls to the area of the code that defines the selected object. SharePoint Designer highlights the code for the selected object.
3 Click [Code]	To switch to Code view.
4 Locate the `<html>` tag	Near the top of the page.
What's the purpose of this element?	
5 Locate the `<head>` tag	
What's the purpose of this element?	
6 Locate the `<body>` tag	
What's the purpose of this element?	
7 Click [Design]	To return to Design view.

The Quick Tag Selector

Explanation

You've already selected page elements by clicking them within a page. Sometimes, depending on how you plan to format a selected element, you might need to select other HTML tags surrounding an element. You can do this by using the Quick Tag Selector, which is displayed by default at the top of the Document window.

The Quick Tag Selector is context-sensitive, meaning that it changes, based on what you select on a page. For example, if you select an image, the Quick Tag Selector highlights the image tag, as shown in Exhibit 1-11. The Quick Tag Selector also shows the elements that precede the selected element. If you want to select the paragraph directly above the image, you could click the `<p>` tag to the left of the `<img>` tag.

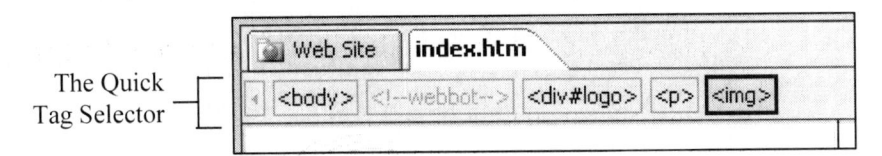

The Quick Tag Selector — [Web Site | index.htm | `<body>` | `<!--webbot-->` | `<div#logo>` | `<p>` | `<img>`]

Exhibit 1-11: The Quick Tag Selector

Do it!

D-2: Selecting page elements

Here's how	Here's why
1 Click anywhere in the paragraph under the Turmeric heading	A small tab with the letter "p" appears at the top of the paragraph. This indicates that the `<p>` tag defines this block of text as a paragraph.
2 Click the tab	To select the entire paragraph.
3 Click the Turmeric heading	Its tab reads "h2," which indicates that the `<h2>` element defines this text as a level-two heading.
4 Click **Welcome**	To select it. Its tab reads "img"—the `<img>` tag defines an image. This image is being used as a heading.
5 Observe the Quick Tag Selector	At the top of the Document window. The `<img>` tag is selected.
6 In the Quick Tag Selector, click **`<h1>`**	(To the left of `<img>`.) To select the element that serves as a container for the image. Nesting the image in an `<h1>` tag identifies the image as the document's top-level heading.
7 Close the document	
8 Choose **File**, **Close Site**	To close the Outlander Web site.

Unit summary: Getting started

Topic A In this topic, you learned a few basics about the **Internet**, the **World Wide Web**, and **HTML**. You learned that HTML is a standard markup language with which Web pages are built.

Topic B In this topic, you identified the components of the **SharePoint Designer interface**, including **toolbars**, **task panes**, the **Document window**, the **Views bar**, and the **status bar**.

Topic C In this topic, you learned basic Web page editing, including inserting and formatting text and images. You also learned how to **preview** a Web page in a browser.

Topic D In this topic, you learned more about **HTML tags**, including **basic HTML syntax** and the fundamental tags that define the structure of a Web page. You also learned how to select elements and tags using the **Quick Tag Selector**.

Independent practice activity

In this activity, you'll experiment briefly with re-organizing task panes in the work area. Then you'll apply basic formatting to text, and add an image to a page. Then you'll preview the page in Internet Explorer, and select content by using the Quick Tag Selector.

1. In the current unit folder, in the Practice folder, open **index.htm**.
2. Reorganize and/or close some of the visible task panes.
3. Reset the task panes to their default layout.
4. Switch to the Hyperlinks view of the site. Observe the link structure for several site pages. (*Hint:* In the Folder List task pane, click several pages.)
5. Switch back to the Folders view.
6. In the home page, in the Monthly Recipes text, apply bold and italic formatting to the text "Outlander Chicken" as shown in Exhibit 1-12.
7. Add the spice_shaker.gif image to the bottom of the right column of text, as shown in Exhibit 1-13. (*Hint:* The spice shaker image is located in the images subfolder.)
8. Save the document and preview the page in Internet Explorer. When you're finished previewing the page, close Internet Explorer to return to SharePoint Designer.
9. Using the Quick Tag Selector, select everything in the right column. (*Hint:* Click to place the insertion point in the right column, and click `<div#rightcolumn>` in the Quick Tag Selector.)
10. Close all open documents.
11. Close the site by choosing **File**, **Close Site**.

Exhibit 1-12: The home page after step 6

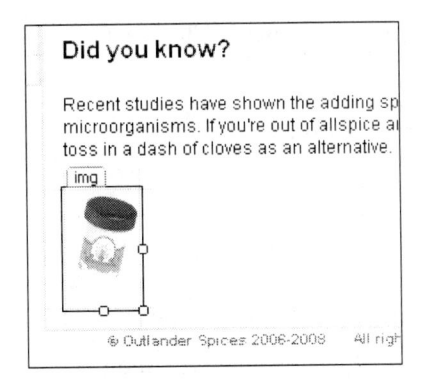

Exhibit 1-13: The home page after step 7

Review questions

1 True or false? In most Web sites, pages are meant to be read in a particular sequence.

2 How can you float a docked task pane?

   A Select the task pane and choose Task Panes, Float Task Pane.

   B Choose Task Panes, <Task Pane Title>, Float Task Pane.

   C Drag the title bar of the task pane away from the other docked task panes.

   D Double-click anywhere inside the task pane.

3 Which are SharePoint Designer site views? (Choose all that apply.)

   A Hyperlinks

   B Images

   C Navigation

   D Remote Web Site

4 Which are ways to add an image to a page? (Choose all that apply.)

   A Place the insertion point on the page and click the Insert Picture from File button in the Standard toolbar.

   B In the Folder List pane, right-click an image and choose Add To Page.

   C Place the insertion point on the page and double-click an image in the Folder List pane.

   D Drag the image from the Folder List pane to the page.

5 True or false? It's generally better to preview your pages directly in SharePoint Designer, rather than preview them in a browser.

6 What are the three most fundamental HTML tags that exist in every Web page?

   A `<title>`, `<head>`, and `<body>`

   B `<html>`, `<head>`, and `<body>`

   C `<start>`, `<body>`, and `<end>`

   D `<html>`, `<head>`, and `<content>`

Unit 2
Web sites

Unit time: 45 minutes

Complete this unit, and you'll know how to:

A Plan the design and structure of a site.

B Create a new one-page site and additional pages and subfolders.

C Create a template with editable regions, set basic page properties, and apply a template to existing pages in a site.

Topic A: Site planning basics

Explanation

When you begin to plan your Web site's design, consider more than your visual design approach. Other factors, like accessibility, structure, navigation, and consistency in multiple browsers, are equally important.

When you start a new Web site, you might be inclined to write the content for the pages first. But it's best to plan your Web site carefully before writing the content. Think about how best to structure your pages and content, how you want to present information, and stylistic concerns such as color scheme and font faces—before you begin work on individual pages. Spend some time defining the audience for the site and the goals you want to accomplish with it.

Basic elements of a site plan

Keep these factors in mind before you begin designing your site:

- **Audience.** Analyze the interests, age, experiences, background, and expectations of your audience. You'll find that many of your later design choices are based on this analysis.
- **Objective.** Set well-defined objectives for your Web site. An objective should be specific, measurable, and realistic.
- **Content.** The content should clearly convey the message of your site and should be relevant for your users. The language, tone, graphics, and level of detail should all be based on your target audience.
- **Site structure.** Finalize the navigation structure at the beginning of the design process. Changing the site structure later can be costly and time consuming.

Basic design elements

You can attract and retain users by designing pages that make it easy for them to find the information they're looking for. You can do this with a blend of colors, graphics, content, and navigational aids. While planning the design, keep the following points in mind:

- **Navigation.** Your navigation scheme should reflect your site's structure, and it should be consistent on every page.
- **Fonts.** Choose fonts that provide optimal readability and that suit your target audience. For example, you might use standard fonts, such as Arial and Times New Roman for a corporate site, but a more playful font, such as Comic Sans MS, for a kids' site.
- **Headings.** Use headings carefully. They should serve as titles or brief descriptors for the content beneath them.
- **Page length.** Break information into manageable chunks. A page that contains excessive text that requires a lot of vertical scrolling can be tedious to your users.
- **Visual contrast.** Make sure your background color and text color have sufficient contrast, so that the text is clear, crisp, and easy to read.
- **Load time.** Use graphics and components conservatively. You can lose visitors if it takes too long for your pages to load.

Do it!

A-1: Discussing design considerations

Questions and answers

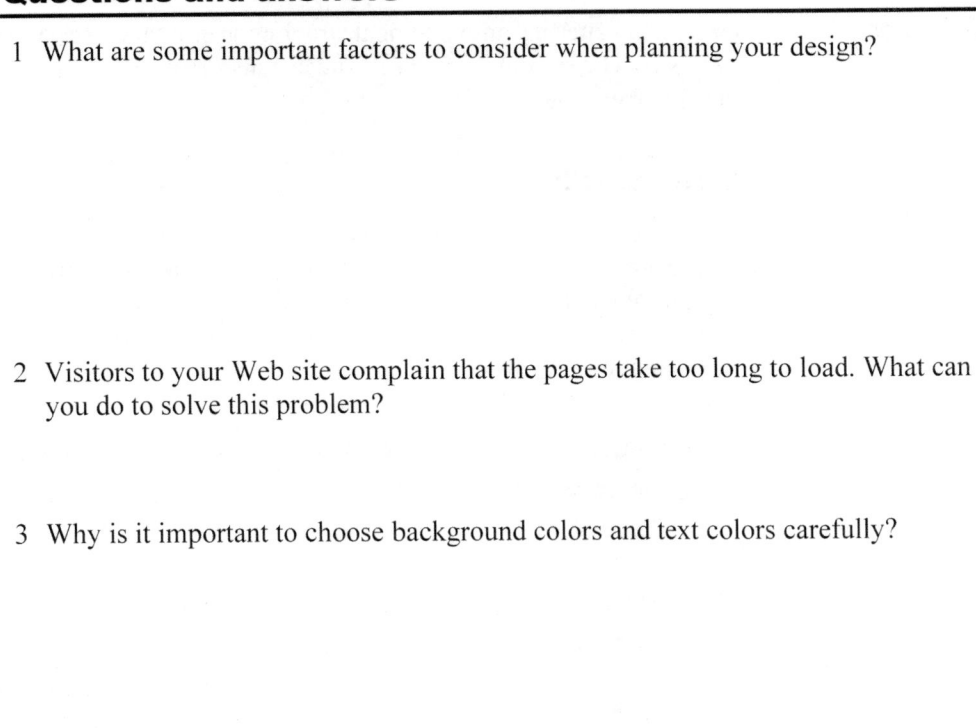

1 What are some important factors to consider when planning your design?

2 Visitors to your Web site complain that the pages take too long to load. What can you do to solve this problem?

3 Why is it important to choose background colors and text colors carefully?

4 Why is it important to break text into logical, manageable chunks?

Topic B: Creating a Web site

Explanation

Organizing site files into a logical structure is critical to the successful operation of your Web site. The structure of a Web site can also impact a developer's ability to maintain the site over time.

Site structure

A well-designed site should have an effective navigation scheme. You need to plan the link relationships between the pages in your site, and organize your site assets into a logical folder structure. Exhibit 2-1 shows a typical Web site folder structure, where all images, styles, templates, and sometimes multimedia files, scripts, and subpages, are stored in their own folders.

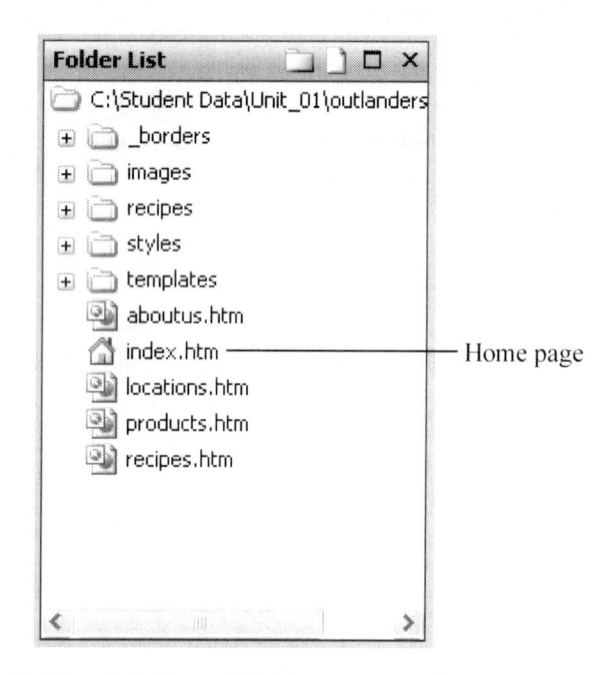

Exhibit 2-1: Typical folder structure for a Web site

The home page

A *home page* is the introductory page of a Web site. It might contain a brief welcome message or a statement that describes the purpose of the Web site. For well-established corporate sites, it might merely provide a teaser graphic or animation, with links to access information within the site. The home page is typically a file named *default.htm* (or *default.html*, *index.htm*, or *index.html*). This is a standard naming convention that most servers use to identify the root page of a site. When you type in an address in your browser, such as www.outlanderspices.com, the default, or "index" page typically loads automatically.

Local sites

When you create a new site, you typically store the site folder locally (somewhere that's easily accessible on your computer's hard drive.) This way, you can test the site before you publish it on the Web. When you complete the site, you can publish it to a remote folder on the Web server that hosts your site.

A *local site* serves as the root directory for your Web site. When defining the site's root folder, don't use the root of your hard drive or the SharePoint Designer application folder.

To create a one-page Web site:

1. Choose File, New. The New dialog box opens.
2. Activate Web Site to view options for creating the new site.
3. In the General category, click One Page Web Site.
4. In the Specify new location of Web site box, enter the file path where you want to create the new site. Click Browse to navigate to the location of the site folder, if one already exists.
5. Click OK to create the site.

You can also create an empty Web site or import an existing site by selecting those options in the New dialog box.

Do it!

B-1: Defining a one-page Web site

Here's how	Here's why
1 Choose **File, New...**	To open the New dialog box. The Page tab is active by default.
2 Activate the **Web Site** tab	The dialog box changes to show options for creating a new Web site. You'll start by creating a one-page Web site. A folder containing images for the site already exists.
3 In the center column, click **One Page Web Site**	One Page Web Site Empty Web Site Import Web Site Wizard To select it.
4 Click **Browse...**	The New Web Site Location dialog box appears.
Navigate to the current unit folder	
Double-click the **Outlander** folder	To open it. This file contains several images and a Microsoft Word document. It doesn't contain any Web pages.
5 Click **Open**	To return to the New dialog box. The file path for the folder is visible in the location box.
6 Click **OK**	To create a Web site with a single blank page.
7 Observe the Folder List pane	The files that comprise the site are listed here. SharePoint Designer creates a new page named default.htm, which is the Web site's home page.
8 Double-click **default.htm**	To open it. The page is currently blank.
9 Drag **spice_month.gif** from the Folder List pane to the page	(To add the image to the page.) The Accessibility Properties dialog box appears. When you insert images, you should specify relevant alternate text so that users who have non-visual browsers can access the content.
In the Alternate text box, type **Spice of the Month**	
Click **OK**	The image appears in the page.
10 Save the document	

New pages and folders

Explanation

To add Web pages and folders to a site, click the New Folder icon or New Page icon at the top of the Folder List pane. For example, clicking the New Page icon adds a new, untitled document to the file list, as shown in Exhibit 2-2. You can then rename the document (or folder) descriptively.

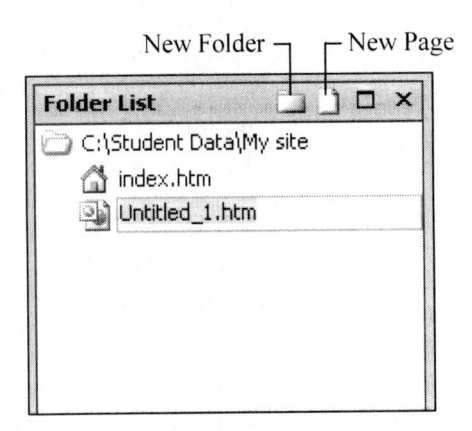

Exhibit 2-2: The Folder List pane

You can also create new pages or folders by using the same icons in the Web Site window, or you can choose File, New to open the New dialog box, and select HTML document from the document types.

Moving documents

As you build a site, you might need to move existing site pages or assets, such as images and media files, into subfolders. You can move files by dragging them in the Folder List pane. It's important that you move documents and assets only from within SharePoint Designer. If you move them outside of SharePoint Designer, your action could result in broken links within your pages.

The Save As command

Sometimes you might want to create a new document based on an existing one. To do so, open the document, and choose File, Save As. In the File name box, specify the name of the new page and click Save.

B-2: Creating new pages and folders

Do it!

Here's how	Here's why
1 Observe the Folder List pane	In addition to the default.htm document, there are images and a text document that were stored in the Outlander folder when you created the site.
2 At the top of the Folder List pane, click ▢	(The New Folder button.) A new folder appears in the list.
Type **images**	
Press ENTER	To create the folder. You'll move all the images to this images subfolder. It's important to move images and documents only within SharePoint Designer. If you move them outside of SharePoint Designer, your action could result in broken links within your pages.
3 In the document, select the **Spice of the Month** image	Click it.
In the Views bar, click Split	To split the window, so that both Code view and Design view are visible.
4 Observe the code for the selected image	By default, SharePoint places images in a `<p>` tag. The `src` attribute indicates the image's file name.
5 Drag **spice_month.gif** to the images subfolder	(In the Folder List pane.) When you move the image, a message box appears briefly, and SharePoint Designer automatically updates the file path in the code.
6 In the Views bar, click Design	To return to Design view.
7 Save the document	
8 Move the remaining images to the images subfolder	(In the Folder List pane.) Move only the files that end with .gif and .jpg. Don't move default.htm or About Us.doc.
9 At the top of the Folder List pane, click the root level folder	[Folder List showing C:\Student Data\... and About Us.doc]
	To make it active. If a subfolder is active when you create a new page, it is placed within that folder. You want these new pages at the root level of the site with the home page.

10	At the top of the Folder List pane, click 🗋	(The New Page button.) A new page appears in the list. You'll create an About Us page and a Locations page.
	Type **aboutus.htm**	
	Press ⏎ ENTER	To rename the document.
11	Create a third page named **locations.htm**	In the Folder List pane, click the New Page button. Then type locations.htm and press Enter.

Topic C: Templates

Explanation

The pages in your site probably share common elements, such as a background image, a banner, or a navigation bar. Instead of recreating these elements on every page, you can create a template document that you can use to create new documents.

Working with templates

Templates can be especially useful when multiple people are developing a site as a team. For example, a developer can create the general design and designate editable regions in the template to hold the content that's unique to each page. Another developer could then add content to the editable regions. Regions not marked as editable can't be modified. This helps ensure consistency across multiple pages. When you need to make changes to certain aspects of the design, you can make those changes to the template file, so that all pages linked to the template are updated automatically. This can make the process of site maintenance much faster and easier.

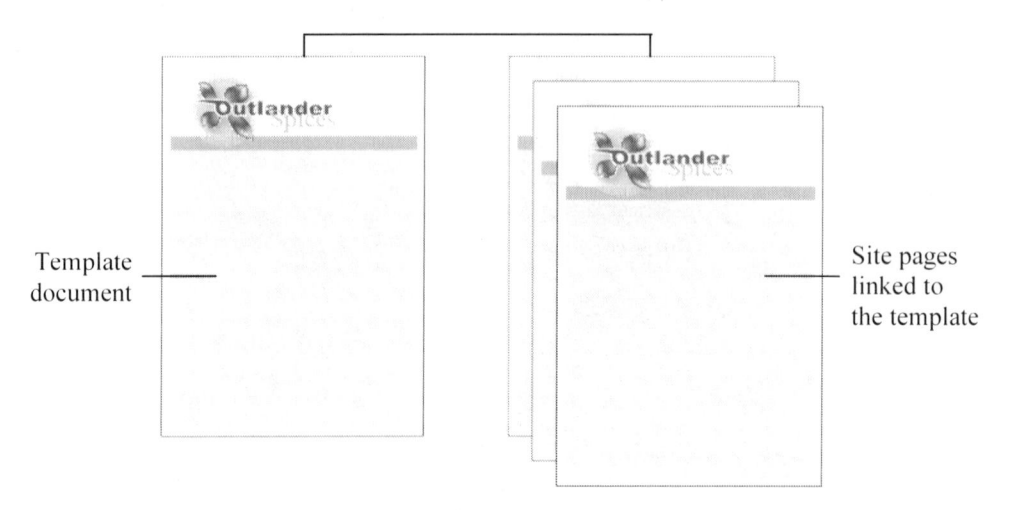

Exhibit 2-3: Pages based on a template

To create a template:

1 Choose File, New to open the New dialog box.
2 In the General category, click Dynamic Web Template.
3 Click OK to create the template, which appears in the work area. (You need to activate Untitled_1.dwt to view the template page.)
4 Save the document with a descriptive name inside the root site folder. Generally, it's a good idea to store the template within its own subfolder (for example, a subfolder titled "templates"). Be sure the document is saved with a .dwt file extension.

Do it!

C-1: Creating a new template

Here's how	Here's why
1 Choose **File, New...**	To open the New dialog box. The Page tab is active by default.
2 In the middle column, select **Dynamic Web Template**	HTML ASPX CSS Master Page **Dynamic Web Template** JavaScript XML Text File
Click **OK**	A new, untitled template document opens. The template looks like a normal HTML document, except that there's a light orange box at the top of the page. This represents the editable area of the page.
3 Choose **File, Save**	The Save As dialog box appears.
Verify that the contents of the Outlander folder are visible	You'll save the template in a separate folder from the rest of the documents.
4 In the top-right corner of the dialog box, click 📁	(The Create New Folder button.) A new folder icon titled "New Folder" appears in the list.
Type **templates** and press ENTER	images aboutus.htm default.htm locations.htm **templates** To rename the folder.
5 Double-click the templates folder	To open it.
6 In the File name box, type **outlander.dwt** and click **Save**	To save the template.

Editable regions

Explanation

Every template must contain at least one editable region, so that pages linked to the template can be altered. By default, SharePoint Designer specifies the document title and the body sections as editable. However, you can edit and change editable regions any way you want. Editable regions within templates and linked documents are outlined with a light orange border. Any content within the border can be manipulated, but anything outside the border can't be selected (except within the template document itself).

If you're working with a template that contains several elements, you might want to specify exactly which areas are editable, and which areas aren't. To create and manage editable areas in a template:

1 Open the template.
2 Choose Format, Dynamic Web Template, Manage Editable Regions to open the Editable Regions dialog box, as shown in Exhibit 2-4.
3 Select the body region, and click Remove to remove the default editable region. By removing the body region, you can now specify exactly which areas of the template to make editable.
4 Click Close to close the dialog box.
5 In the template, select the content you want to be editable.
6 Choose Format, Dynamic Web Template, Manage Editable Regions to open the Editable Regions dialog box again.
7 In the Region name box, enter a descriptive name for the editable content, and click Add. The new editable region appears in the list.
8 Click Close to close the dialog box.
9 If necessary, repeat the process to define any other editable regions in the template. You'll need to select the area of the page you want to be editable before you open the Editable Regions dialog box.

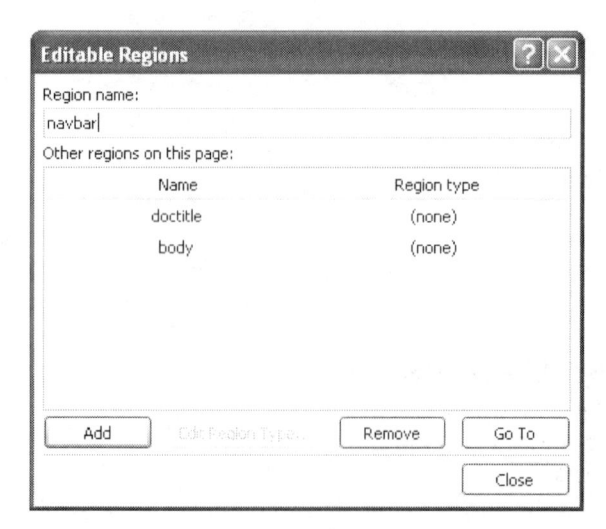

Exhibit 2-4: The Editable Regions dialog box

Web sites **2–13**

Do it!

C-2: Defining editable regions

Here's how	Here's why
1 Choose **Format**, **Dynamic Web Template**, **Manage Editable Regions…**	The Editable Regions dialog box opens. You'll add a logo and navigation bar text to the template, and redefine the area below the elements as editable. To do this, you'll remove the default editable region named "body."
2 Click **body**	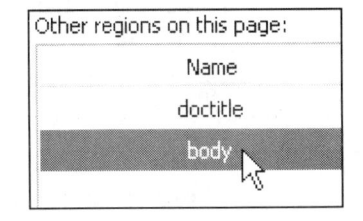 *(Other regions on this page: Name — doctitle, body)* You'll remove this default editable region.
Click **Remove**	
3 Click **Close**	To close the dialog box. Next, you'll add the logo and navigation bar text.
4 In the Folder List pane, expand the images subfolder	
Drag **logo.gif** inside the div section, as shown	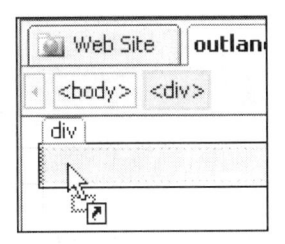 *(Web Site outlan… <body> <div> div)* The Accessibility Properties dialog box appears.
In the Alternate text box, type **Outlander logo**	To indicate to non-visual browsers that the image is a logo.
Click **OK**	The image is inserted in the template.
5 Click under the image	To place the insertion point below the image.
Beneath the logo, type **Home | About Us | Locations | Products | Recipes | Contact Us**	 *(Home | About Us | Locations)* To create the text that will serve as a navigation bar. SharePoint Designer automatically inserts the text in a <p> tag.

6	Click below the navigation bar	To place the insertion point. You'll define the area below the navigation bar as an editable region.
7	Choose **Format**, **Dynamic Web Template**, **Manage Editable Regions...**	To open the Editable Regions dialog box.
	In the Region name box, enter **Content**	
	Click **Add**	To add the new editable region. It now appears in the list, below the existing editable region.
8	Click **Close**	Next, you'll add a copyright statement below the editable region.
9	Click below the Content region	To place the insertion point.
	Type **Copyright Outlander Spices 2006-2008. All rights reserved.**	
10	Save the template	

Page properties

Explanation

By default, SharePoint Designer creates all new pages with a white background. However, you can modify the default page properties to change the look of a page in several ways. For example, you can change the background color, set page margins, set hyperlink colors, and add page titles. If you specify page properties for a template, any pages linked to the template share those properties. To adjust page properties, right-click anywhere on an open page, and choose Page Properties to open the Page Properties dialog box.

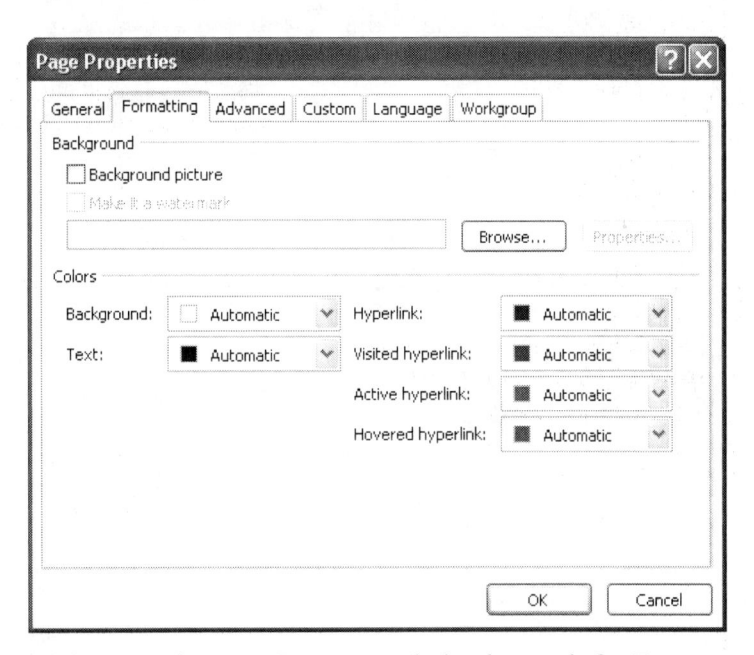

Exhibit 2-5: The Page Properties dialog box with the Formatting tab activated

Page titles

Every page in a site should have a unique title. The page title doesn't appear on the page as content. Instead, it appears in the title bar of the Browser window. To add a unique page title, activate the General tab of the Page Properties dialog box and enter the title in the Title box.

Page margins

Various browsers apply their own default Web page margins. A *margin* is the space between a page's content and the edges of the browser window. (Margins can also exist between individual elements.) Most browsers apply between 10 and 15 pixels of space to establish a default margin. If you don't specify your own page margins, then your page margins are determined by a browser's default setting, and because many browsers apply different margins, this can lead to inconsistent and unpredictable results in your page layouts.

To ensure that your Web pages are displayed consistently, it's important that you set a page margin for all your pages. You can even set your page margins to zero, so that some of your content, such as a navigation bar or header logo, can appear flush with the edge of the browser window. You can then apply margins to large content sections or individual elements to ensure that other content has ample offset space from the browser window and other page elements. To set page margins, enter the margin values you want in the Margin boxes within the Advanced category.

Background images and colors

It's common for designers to use background images or to change the background color of a page to enhance a page's appearance. When you apply a background image, the browser automatically repeats the image from left to right and downward to occupy the entire page. This is called *tiling*. In general, you should try not to use individual images for a tiled background, as the image will likely distract from the page content, as demonstrated in Exhibit 2-6.

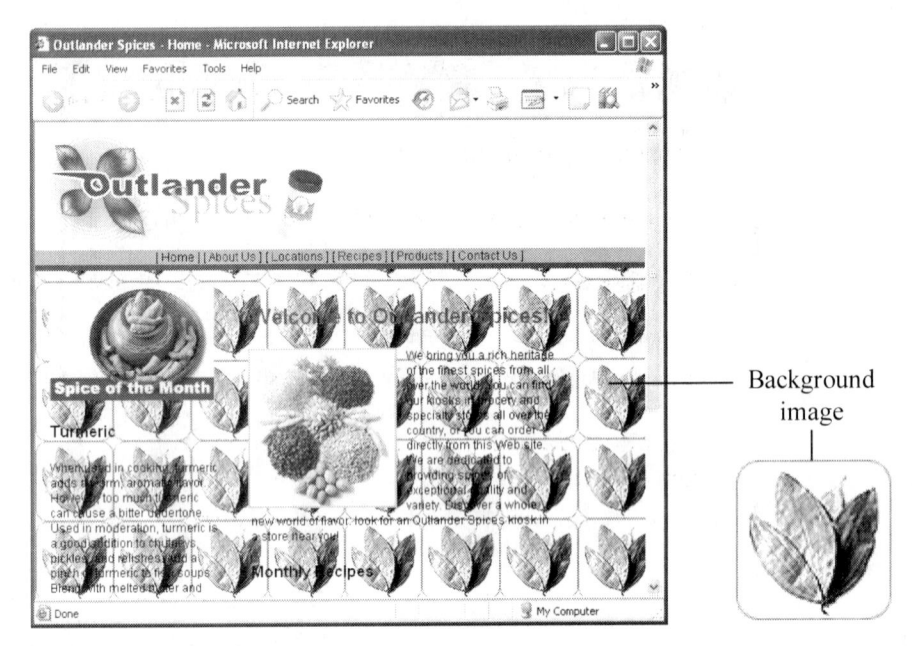

Exhibit 2-6: An example of a distracting tiled background image

Instead, you can often create consistent background patterns by using a very small pattern image. When the image is tiled, it gives the appearance of a solid background, as demonstrated in Exhibit 2-7.

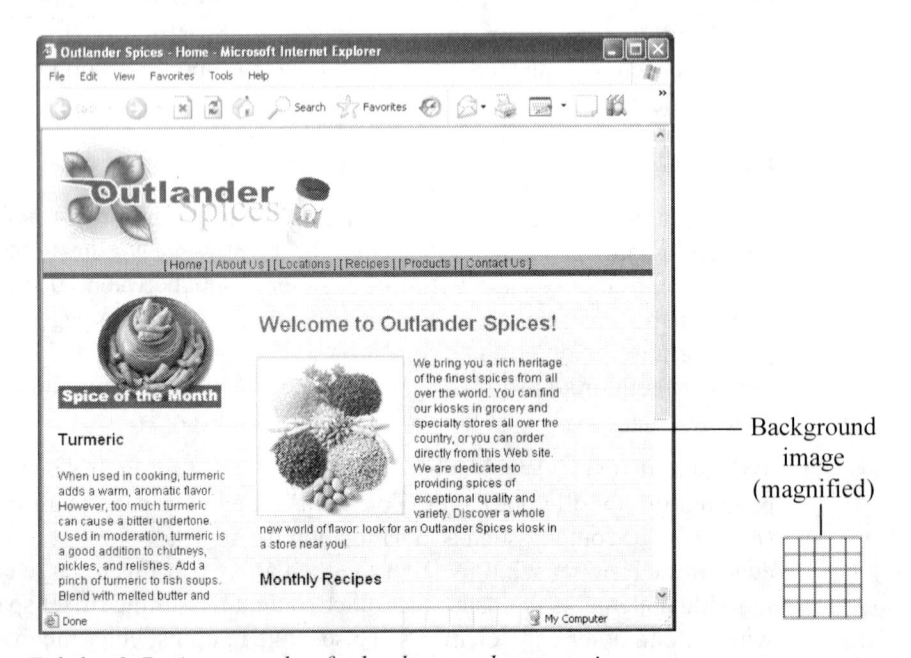

Exhibit 2-7: An example of a background pattern image

Web sites **2-17**

To apply a background image, activate the Formatting tab in the Page Properties dialog box, and check Background image. Then, either enter the path to the image, or click Browse to navigate to the image. To apply a background color, select a color from the Background list.

Do it!

C-3: Setting basic page properties

Here's how	Here's why
1 Right-click anywhere on the page and choose **Page Properties…**	To open the Page Properties dialog box. You'll remove the default page margins and add a tiling background image.
Activate the Formatting tab	
2 Check **Background picture**	
3 Click **Browse…**	The Select Picture Background dialog box appears.
Navigate to the images subfolder	In the current unit folder.
4 Select **background.gif**, and click **Open**	Background ☑ Background picture ☐ Make it a watermark ../images/background.gif
	The file path for the image appears in the Background image box. You'll also remove the default page margins so that content abuts the edges of a browser window.
5 Activate the Advanced tab	
6 In each margin box, enter **0**	Top Margin: 0 Left Margin: 0 Bottom Margin: 0 Right Margin: 0
7 Click **OK**	To close the dialog box. The page now uses the tiling green background image, and the default margins are removed.
8 Save the template	

Applying templates

Explanation

When you apply a template to a page that has existing content, you need to assign the content to the template's editable region(s). However, when creating a new page based on the template, the new page simply shows the basic contents of the template.

To create a new page from a template:

1 Choose File, New to open the New dialog box.
2 In the General category, select Create from Dynamic Web Template.
3 Click OK. The Attach Dynamic Web Template dialog box appears.
4 Navigate to the location of your template and click Open. An alert box appears, indicating that the page has been updated.
5 Click Close to close the dialog box. The new page with the template attached is visible in the work area.

To apply a template to an existing page:

1 Open the page, or Ctrl-click multiple documents in the Folder List pane.
2 Choose Format, Dynamic Web Template, Attach Dynamic Web Template. The Attach Dynamic Web Template dialog box appears.
3 Navigate to the location of the template and click Open. A message box appears. Click Yes.
4 If the page contains content, the Match Editable Regions dialog box appears.
5 Select an editable region to which to assign the existing content. (Unless you've created multiple edited regions, the body region is the only region available.)
6 Click OK. An alert box appears, indicating that the page has been updated.
7 Click Close to close the alert box. If you applied the template to an open page, the results are visible on the page. If you applied the template to multiple pages in the Folder List pane, the results are visible when you open the documents.

Do it!

C-4: Applying a template

Here's how	Here's why
1 Switch to the Home page	At the top of the document window, activate default.htm.
2 Choose **Format, Dynamic Web Template, Attach Dynamic Web Template…**	To open the Attach Dynamic Web Template dialog box.
In the upper-right corner, click	To go up one level in the folder structure. The templates folder is now visible.
Open the templates folder	
Select **outlander.dwt** and click **Open**	A message box appears.
Click **Yes**	The Match Editable Regions dialog box appears. Because the page contains an image, you need to specify the region in the template where you want the image to appear. In this template, there's only one editable region.

Web sites **2–19**

3	Click **(Content)**	To select the region.
	Click **OK**	An alert box appears, indicating that one file was updated, in reference to the home page.
4	Click **Close**	To close the alert box. The home page now uses the components of the outlander template. The logo, navigation bar text, and copyright text are all part of the page now.
5	Observe the top-right corner of the document window	templates/outlander.dwt

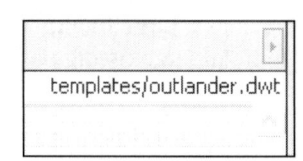

The page indicates the template file path.

	Click the logo	To try to select it. The pointer changes to a circle with a line through it. The image is within a non-editable region of the template, so you can't select it.
6	In the Folder List pane, select **aboutus.htm**	
	Press `CTRL`	So that you can select multiple files.
	Select **locations.htm**	
7	Choose **Format**, **Dynamic Web Template**, **Attach Dynamic Web Template…**	To open the Attach Dynamic Web Template dialog box.
8	Select **outlander.dwt** and click **Open**	A message box appears.
	Click **Yes**	The same message appears for the second file you're attaching.
	Click **Yes**	The alert box indicates that two files were updated. Because neither page contains any content, you didn't need to assign content to editable regions.
9	Click **Close**	
10	Open **aboutus.htm**	The non-editable items in the template are visible on the page.
11	Save and close all open documents	If prompted, click Yes to update files using the template.
12	Choose **File**, **Close Site**	To close the Outlander Web site.

Unit summary: Web sites

Topic A   In this topic, you learned the basics of planning the design and structure of a site.

Topic B   In this topic, you created a new one-page site in SharePoint Designer. Next, you generated additional pages and folders, and you organized documents by using the Folder List pane.

Topic C   In this topic, you created a **template document** and set basic **page properties** for it, such as a **page background** and **page margins**. Then you learned how to apply a template to existing pages in the site.

Independent practice activity

In this activity, you'll create a new one-page site based on an existing site folder. Then you'll create new subfolders to organize some of the documents, and create some new site pages. You'll create a template and set up basic page properties for it, and lastly, you'll apply the template to multiple pages.

1. In the Practice folder (in the current unit folder), there are several images and a Word document. Create a new one-page Web site based on the Practice folder. (*Hint:* When you create the new site, navigate to the Practice folder to use it for the root folder.)

2. Within the new site, create a new subfolder named **images**, and move all the image files to the subfolder. (The image files include everything except default.htm and About Us.doc.)

3. Create two new pages for the site. Name the pages **aboutus.htm** and **locations.htm**. (*Hint:* Be sure to click the root folder in the Folder List pane to keep from creating the documents in the images subfolder.)

4. Create a new Dynamic Web Template document. Name the template **outlander.dwt** and store it in a new subfolder named **templates**.

5. Remove the default Body editable region from the template.

6. Add the **toplogo.gif** image, enter navigation bar text, and enter a copyright statement, as shown in Exhibit 2-8.

7. Apply the **Background.gif** image as a background image in the template. Also, set the page margins to 0 (zero), as shown in Exhibit 2-9.

8. Create a new editable region between the navigation bar text and the copyright statement, as shown in Exhibit 2-10. (*Hint:* Be sure to click the "p" tab to select the `<p>` tags before you create the editable region.)

9. Save and apply the template to all the pages in the site.

10. Close any open documents and close the site.

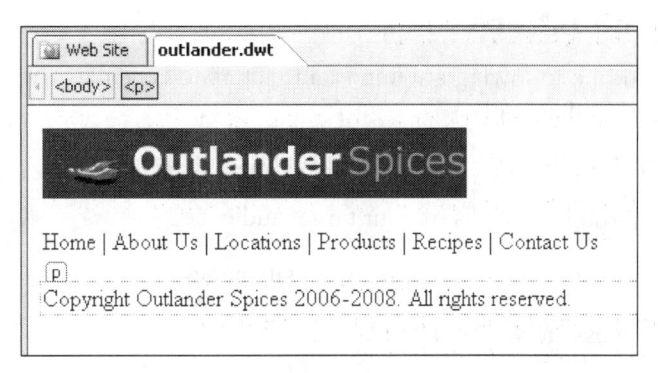

Exhibit 2-8: The template after step 6

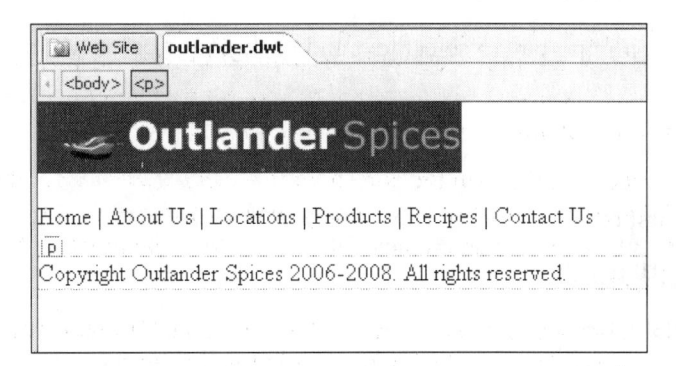

Exhibit 2-9: The template after step 7

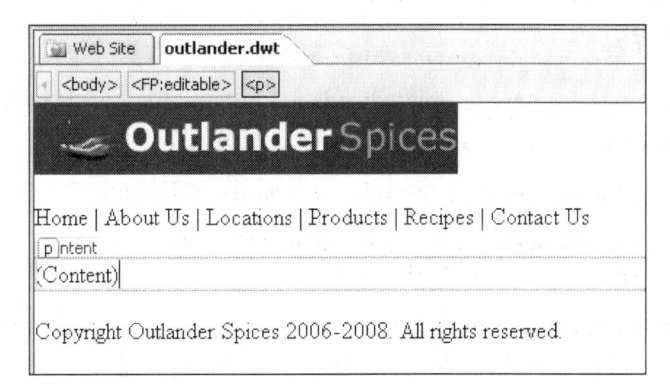

Exhibit 2-10: The template after step 8

Review questions

1 Which of the following are important factors to consider when planning a Web site? (Choose all that apply.)

   A How the site pages look when printed on paper

   B A thorough analysis of your target audience

   C The navigation structure between site pages

   D The message your content conveys

   E The overall objective of the Web site

   F How cool the site looks

2 Why is it important to select text and background colors carefully?

3 The first page you see when you view a Web site is typically referred to as the:

   A startup page

   B first page

   C main page

   D home page

   E interstitial

4 True or false? Every template needs to contain at least one editable region.

5 Why is it often a good idea to set your own page margins?

6 When you insert a background image, by default, the image

   A repeats, or "tiles" horizontally.

   B repeats, or "tiles" vertically.

   C repeats, or "tiles" horizontally and vertically.

   D repeats, or "tiles" diagonally.

Unit 3
Text formatting

Unit time: 50 minutes

Complete this unit, and you'll know how to:

A Import text, convert line breaks into paragraphs, and insert spaces and symbols.

B Apply structural formatting to text and create lists.

C Create an external style sheet and create element and class styles.

Topic A: Text basics

Explanation

In addition to entering text directly into a document, you can also add text from other files, such as other Web pages or Word documents.

Adding content from another source

To import text, simply select and copy the desired text and then paste the text into the desired location on the page. If the text you're pasting has styles applied to it, a Paste Options icon appears at the end of the text. Click the icon to view a list of options for the text, as shown in Exhibit 3-1. You can choose to keep the source formatting, remove formatting, keep HTML only, or keep text only.

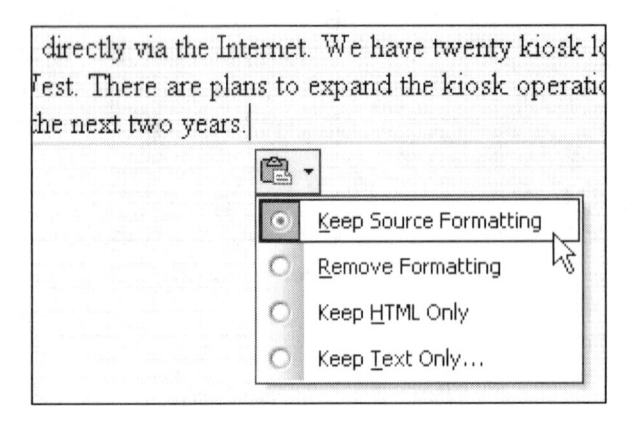

Exhibit 3-1: The Paste Options drop-down list

If you're importing text and you know you don't want to include any previously applied formatting, you can use the Paste Text command. Choose Edit, Paste Text to open the Paste Text dialog box, as shown in Exhibit 3-2. You can configure how to import the text before it's added to the page. You can select to add the text as plain text, use `<pre>` tags to maintain paragraphs, or use line breaks to control paragraphs. The advantage of using the Paste Text command is that it reduces excess tags within the text that could be generated if you were to paste the text and then use the Paste Options icon to remove the formatting. It provides a cleaner method for adding text.

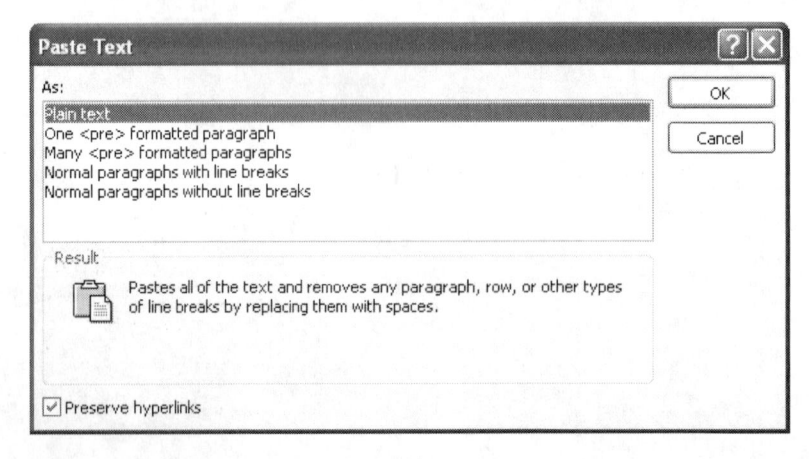

Exhibit 3-2: The Paste Text dialog box

Text formatting 3–3

Do it!

A-1: Importing text

Here's how	Here's why
1 Choose **File**, **Open Site...**	
Navigate to the current unit folder	
Open the Outlander folder	The folders and pages in the site appear in the work area.
2 Open aboutus.htm	The page contains the standard content from the Outlander template. You'll add text from a Word document to the page.
3 In the Folder List pane, double-click **About Us.doc**	(To open it.) This document was created using Microsoft Word. If Word is installed on your computer, it starts and then opens the document. If Word isn't installed, the document opens in Word Pad.
4 Press CTRL + A	To select all the text in the document.
Press CTRL + C	To copy the text.
Close Word (or Word Pad)	Without saving any changes.
5 In aboutus.htm, select **(Content)**	
	(The editable region is outlined in light orange.) You'll delete this default content and replace it with the content from the Word document.
Press DELETE	To delete the default content.
6 Choose **Edit**, **Paste Text...**	The Paste Text dialog box appears.
Select **Normal paragraphs with line breaks**	
Click **OK**	The text is added to the page.
7 Save the document	Click the Save button.

Line breaks and paragraph breaks

Explanation

In a word processor, you use line breaks and paragraph breaks to mark the end of a line. A line break forces text to begin on a new line, but within the same paragraph. A paragraph break begins a new line and also marks the end of a paragraph. These codes are usually hidden in a word processor document but can be displayed, if desired, as shown in Exhibit 3-3. SharePoint Designer uses its own visual cues to indicate line breaks and paragraph breaks.

> This·sentence·ends·in·a·line·break.↵
> This·second·sentence·ends·in·a·line·break.↵
> All·three·lines·are·part·of·the·same·paragraph.¶

> This·sentence·ends·in·a·paragraph·break.¶
> This·second·sentence·is·a·separate·paragraph.¶

Exhibit 3-3: Line breaks (top) and paragraph breaks (bottom) in a word processor

Many of SharePoint Designer's text formatting tools and shortcuts are paragraph-based, which means that text formatting is applied to an entire paragraph. Therefore, if you apply paragraph formatting to text that ends in a line break, the text after the line break is affected as well. Depending on how you want to format text, you might need to convert line breaks to paragraph breaks or vice versa.

- To convert a line break to a paragraph break, select the line break and press Enter.
- To convert a paragraph break to a line break, select the paragraph break, press and hold Shift, and press Enter.

Show Formatting marks

By default, line break marks, paragraph marks, and spaces aren't visible on a page. You can make them visible by clicking the Show Formatting Marks button on the Standard toolbar. To hide them, click the button again.

You can also show specific formatting marks by selecting them from the drop-down list to the right of the Show Formatting Marks button or by choosing them from the View, Formatting Marks submenu.

Do it!

A-2: Changing line breaks to paragraph breaks

Here's how	Here's why
1 Scroll to the top of the page	(If necessary.) You'll separate headings from text with paragraph breaks so you can format them. It's sometimes easier to work with line and paragraph breaks if you make them visible first.
2 Choose **View**, **Formatting Marks**, **Show**	To make formatting marks visible.

Text formatting 3–5

3 At the top of the page, select **All Spiced Up!**, as shown

This text is on a separate line but is still part of the paragraph that follows it.

4 In the Views bar, click [Split]

To display Code view and Design view simultaneously. The selection is also highlighted in Code view.

In Code view, observe the surrounding HTML tags

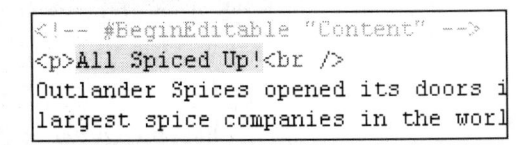

The text is defined with a paragraph tag and ends with a line break tag. (The `<p>` tag indicates the start of a paragraph and the `<br />` tag is a line break.) You need to make this line of text its own paragraph by converting the line break to a closing paragraph tag.

5 In Design view, click the line break mark

To select it. You'll replace this line break with a paragraph break.

6 Press [← ENTER]

To replace the line break with a paragraph break.

7 Verify the result in Code view

A closing paragraph tag (`</p>`) now marks the end of the text "All Spiced Up!" and an opening paragraph tag now marks the beginning of the next line of text.

8 Verify the result in Design view

A paragraph mark appears at the end of the line, and a larger space separates the title and the text.

9 Convert the remaining line breaks to paragraphs

Click to select each line break mark and press Enter.

10 Choose **View**, **Formatting Marks**, **Show**

To disable formatting marks.

Spaces

Explanation

In HTML code, only one blank space between words is recognized. If you add more than one space between words in Code view, the text in Design view (and in a browser) isn't affected—there remains only one space between each word. To add extra spaces in text on a Web page, you need to use the *non-breaking space* character (` `) in the code. You can do this by adding spaces in Design view (by pressing the Spacebar) or by manually adding the necessary non-breaking space character codes in Code view.

Do it!

A-3: Inserting spaces

Here's how	Here's why
1 In Design view, scroll to the bottom of the page	(If necessary.) To view the copyright text. You'll add spaces between each sentence in the text. However, the copyright statement is stored in the template document.
2 Open the Outlander template	(In the templates subfolder.) The template opens in Split view.
In Code view, scroll down to view the copyright statement	
3 Place the insertion point, as shown	`2006-2008.`|`All rights` You'll insert spaces after the copyright notice.
4 Press SPACEBAR four times	To insert four spaces.
5 Click in Design view	To refresh the document. The ordinary spaces entered in the HTML code have no effect. To add spaces to text by using the Spacebar, you must add the spaces in Design view.
6 In Design view, place the insertion point as shown	`2006-2008.`|`All rights reserved.` If necessary.
Press SPACEBAR four times	
7 Verify the result in Code view	`08.     All` Each time you add a space, SharePoint Designer inserts a non-breaking space character.

Symbols

Explanation

Some characters that you might need in your content aren't included on a computer keyboard, such as the copyright symbol (©) or foreign language characters, such as the umlaut (ü), shown above the letter "u" here. You can insert these symbols in a Web page by using the Insert Symbol dialog box.

To insert a symbol:

1. Place the insertion point where you want to insert the symbol.
2. Choose Insert, Symbol to open the Symbol dialog box, shown in Exhibit 3-4.
3. If necessary, select the Font you want from the Font list.
4. If necessary, select a symbol subset from the Subset list.
5. Scroll through the list of symbols and click the symbol you want to insert. A list of recently used symbols also appears near the bottom of the dialog box.
6. Click Insert to insert the symbol.
7. Click Close to close the dialog box.

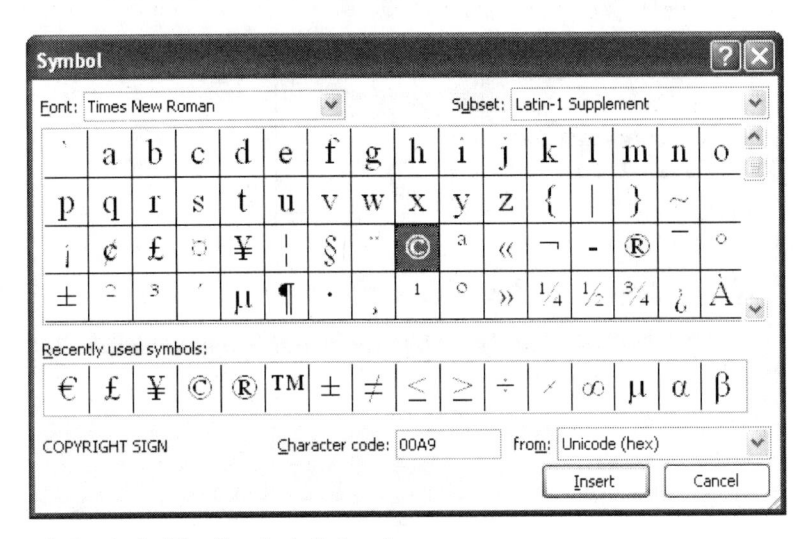

Exhibit 3-4: The Symbol dialog box

Auto CSS settings

Cascading Style Sheets (CSS) is the standard style language for Web content. Some of the default CSS settings in SharePoint Designer might interfere with global CSS styles (shared styles that apply to multiple pages to establish consistency). Inserting symbols is one example of this. When you insert a symbol, SharePoint Designer automatically generates an internal CSS style in order to maintain any font formatting specified for it. For example, if you select Times New Roman in the Font list in the Symbols dialog box, SharePoint Designer creates an internal CSS style that applies the Times New Roman font, even if you change the font for the rest of the text in the paragraph.

If you want to be able to change the formatting for a symbol, you can go into the code and delete the CSS formatting applied to it, or you can adjust a setting in SharePoint Designer before you insert the symbol that prevents SharePoint Designer from producing the CSS style.

To prevent SharePoint Designer from generating CSS styles automatically, right-click Auto in the status bar. From the menu that appears, choose Mode, Manual, as shown in Exhibit 3-5. This setting remains in effect until you switch it back.

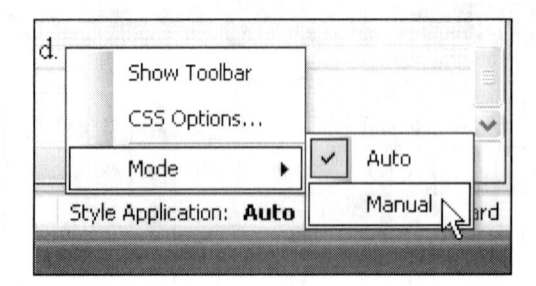

Exhibit 3-5: Changing the CSS style application mode in the status bar

Do it!

A-4: Inserting a symbol

Here's how	Here's why
1 In Design view, scroll to the bottom of the template	(If necessary.) You'll replace the word Copyright with a copyright symbol.
2 Double-click the word **Copyright**	
	To select it.
3 Choose **Insert, Symbol…**	To open the Symbol dialog box.
Observe the Font list	The default font applied to the text (Times New Roman) is the selected font in the list.
4 Scroll to locate the copyright symbol and click once, as shown	
	(To select it.) The copyright symbol is near the top of the list, at the end of the alphabet.
Click **Insert**	
Click **Close**	To close the dialog box. The text "Copyright" is replaced with a copyright symbol.
5 Observe the copyright symbol in Code view	`<span class="style1">©</span>`
	In the code, the copyright symbol is contained in a `<span>` tag. By default, SharePoint Designer applies internal CSS styles to text that has a font applied to it. In this case, you don't want SharePoint Designer to create a style automatically. You want the copyright symbol to be formatted the same as the rest of the text in the paragraph.
Press CTRL + Z	To undo the change, and convert the copyright symbol back to the copyright text.

6 In the status bar, right-click **Auto** and choose **Mode**, **Manual**	To prevent SharePoint Designer from automatically generating CSS styles. You'll now re-insert the symbol without creating a CSS style.
Close the Style Application toolbar	
7 Verify that the Copyright text is still selected	
Choose **Insert**, **Symbol…**	To open the Symbol dialog box.
8 In the Font box, triple-click **Times New Roman**	To select it.
Press ← BACKSPACE	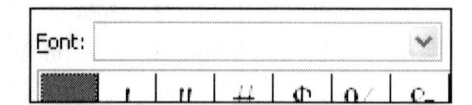 To remove the font formatting.
9 Insert the copyright symbol	Select it from the main list, as before, and not from the Recently used symbols list.
Click **Close**	To close the dialog box. This time, the copyright symbol is added without any CSS formatting. Now, if you change the font formatting for the entire paragraph, the copyright symbol is formatted too.
10 Save the template	Click Yes and Close in the alert boxes to update all documents linked to the template.

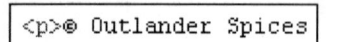

Topic B: Structural formatting

Explanation

You can use headings, paragraphs, and other structural elements to organize a Web page into a logical hierarchy, which can make your pages more searchable, easier to read, and easier for other developers to modify. A well-designed page structure can also make it easier to design and arrange your page content and make that content accessible to users with alternative browsing devices.

Headings

When you're creating a Web page with a lot of content, think of it as a traditional outline, and structure the content accordingly. HTML provides a set of six headings that you can use to structure text headings in your documents. The tags for these headings are `<h1>` through `<h6>`. They each have their own default formatting. Browsers display all headings in bold text by default, and they appear in various font sizes. The `<h1>` tag applies the largest default font size, and the `<h6>` applies the smallest default font size. For example, if you're creating a page intended to deliver company news, an effective structure might look something like this:

```
<h1>Company News</h1>
<p>First paragraph of Company News...</p>
<p>Second paragraph of Company News...</p>
<h2>Sub-heading of Company News</h2>
<p>First paragraph of sub-topic...</p>
```

To apply structural tags to existing content, click to place the insertion point in the heading you want to format, and then select the desired heading style (Heading 1 through Heading 6) from the Styles list in the Common toolbar, as shown in Exhibit 3-6.

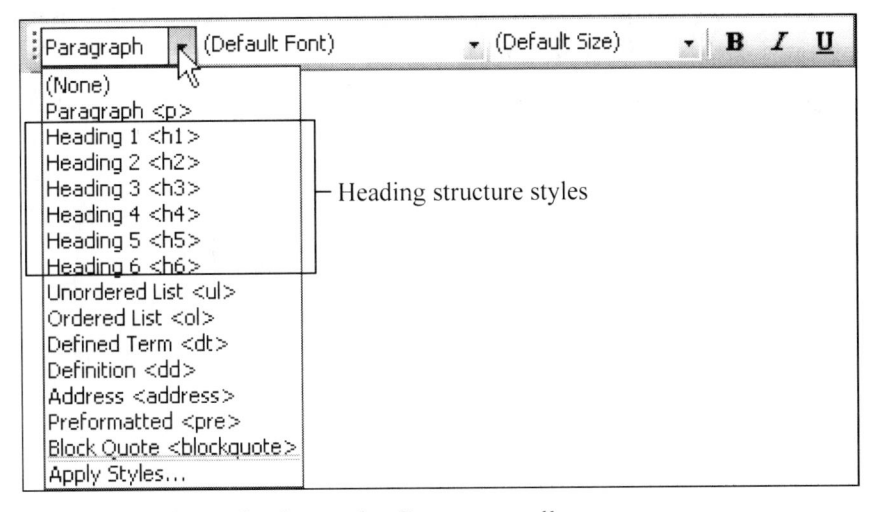

Exhibit 3-6: The Styles list in the Common toolbar

When you're creating your document structure, don't focus on how each element appears in the browser—you can change that later. Instead, think about how best to define the content you're working with, creating a logical arrangement of headings, paragraphs, and lists. You can customize the styles of any HTML tag by using CSS.

Do it!

B-1: Applying headings

Here's how	Here's why
1 Switch to aboutus.htm	Activate the aboutus.htm tab.
In Design view, scroll to the top of the page	If necessary.
2 Click the heading **All Spiced Up!**	
3 In the Common toolbar, from the Style list, select **Heading 1 <h1>**	To format the text as a level-one heading.
In Code view, observe the heading code	```<!-- #BeginEditable "Conter <h1>All Spiced Up!</h1> <p>Outlander Spices opened``` The text is now enclosed in `<h1>` tags to define it as a level-one heading.
4 Format "About our spices" as a level-one heading	(Scroll down, if necessary.) Click in the text to place the insertion point and choose Heading 1 <h1> from the Styles list in the Formatting toolbar.
5 Click in the paragraph that begins with "About our spice blends…"	To place the insertion point.
6 From the Style list, select **Heading 2 <h2>**	To format the text as a level-two heading. The text is large, but not as large as the level-one headings.
7 Save the document	

Lists

Explanation

Lists are another type of structural formatting that you can apply to text. There are three types of lists you can create: unordered lists, ordered lists, and definition lists. In an unordered list, a bullet, circle, square, or other icon precedes each list item. By default, an unordered list uses bullets, as shown in Exhibit 3-7. Use an unordered list when the sequence of the list items isn't important or relevant.

> Our most popular spices include:
> - Bay leaf
> - Cinnamon
> - Coriander
> - Nutmeg
> - Turmeric

Exhibit 3-7: An example of an unordered list

In an ordered list, as shown in Exhibit 3-8, a number or letter indicates each item's order in the list. By default, ordered lists are numbered 1, 2, 3, and so on. You can also choose Alphabet Large (A, B, C), Alphabet Small (a, b, c), Roman Large (I, II, III), or Roman Small (i, ii, iii). Use an ordered list when the sequence of items is important.

> Directions:
> 1. Whisk the yogurt with the paste. Mix well.
> 2. Heat the oil, reduce the heat, and then add onions, ginger and garlic.
> 3. Add the potatoes and fry until golden brown.
> 4. Add the yogurt paste.
> 5. Cook for 5 minutes.
> 6. Add ¾ cup of warm water. Bring to a boil and reduce heat.
> 7. Cook until the potatoes are tender and the gravy is thick.

Exhibit 3-8: An example of an ordered list

You can also create a definition list, which doesn't use bullets or numbers. Instead, a definition list is meant to structure terms and their definitions, for use in glossaries, frequently asked question (FAQ) pages, or similar contexts. Each definition is indented beneath its term, as shown in Exhibit 3-9. This indentation is the only default formatting that browsers apply to a definition list.

> Cinnamon
> > Cinnamon is one of our most popular spices, due to its sweet flavor and prominent role in baked goods and candies. Cinnamon is also wonderful in stews and sauces.
>
> Nutmeg
> > Nutmeg comes from the seed of a tropical tree. It has a sweet, rich and aromatic flavor that complements meats, vegetables, tomato sauces, and baked goods.

Exhibit 3-9: An example of a definition list

To apply list formatting to existing text, select the text, and then select a list structure style from the Style list in the Common toolbar. After you've formatted text as a list, you can also format some of the text as a nested list, if necessary. A *nested list* is a list inside another list. For example, a step in a list of instructions might require its own list of substeps. To create a nested list, select the text you want to format as a nested list, and click either the Increase Indent or Decrease Indent buttons in the Common toolbar.

Do it!

B-2: Creating lists

Here's how	Here's why
1 From the recipes subfolder, open Potatoes.htm Switch to Design view	You'll convert the existing text to ordered and unordered lists.
2 Select all the text between the Ingredients and Directions sub-headings	Ingredients¶ Potatoes, washed and quartered 2·½·cups¶ Oil·½·cup¶ Onions·chopped·½·cup¶ Yogurt·½·cup¶ Dry·roast·and·grind·to·a·paste·with·a·little·water¶ Almonds,·blanched·peeled·and·sliced·3·tbsp¶ Outlander·Spices·Cinnamon·powder:·1·½·tsp¶ Outlander·Spices·Nutmeg·powder·1·½·tsp¶ Outlander·Spices·Coriander·powder·1·½·tsp¶ Outlander·Spices·Red·chili·powder:·3·tsp¶ Garlic·paste·2·tsp¶ Ginger·paste·2·tsp¶ **Directions:**¶

3 From the Style list, select **Unordered List <ul>**

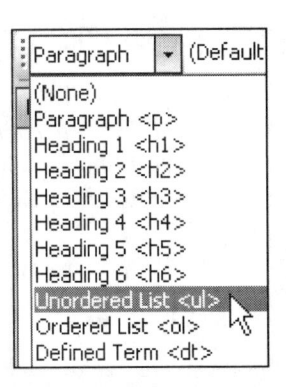

All the paragraphs are converted to items in an unordered list, which is a more appropriate structure for this particular content.

Switch to Code view

Observe the unordered list code

Each item in the list is defined by the `<li>` tag, and every list item is nested inside the `<ul>` tag, which is the unordered list tag.

Switch to Design view

4 Select the three paragraphs under the Directions heading

(Scroll down if necessary.) You'll convert these paragraphs to an ordered list.

5 From the Style list, select **Ordered List <ol>**

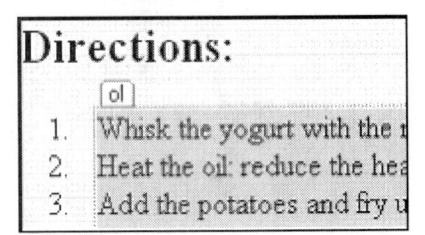

The text is now an ordered list with three sequential steps.

6 Select the ingredient items from Almonds to Red chili powder, as shown

(Scroll up to the unordered list.) You'll indent these list items to create a nested list.

7 In the Common toolbar, click

(The Increase Indent button.) The items are indented and have a different default bullet style.

8 Save and close the document

Topic C: Cascading Style Sheets

Explanation

Cascading Style Sheets (CSS) is the standard style language for the Web, and it allows you to control how HTML elements appear in a browser. For example, you can use CSS to define how `<h1>` elements appear on all the pages in your site or on an individual page.

Applying CSS styles

You can change the default styles that browsers apply to certain HTML elements. For example, by default, browsers make level-one headings large and bold. You can use CSS to make all level-one headings a particular color, font face, and font size, as well as apply other styles. You can control elements of page design and layout, such as margins, spacing, and borders. What makes CSS especially powerful is that you can link multiple pages to a style sheet so that you can make changes to an unlimited number of Web pages by simply updating rules in the style sheet file.

This can save a lot of time when you need to update your site's design, and it ensures a consistent appearance across all pages. With CSS, you can also create more efficient pages, because the style rules are listed only once in a style sheet, rather than repeated in every HTML page.

Internal and external style sheets

Style sheets can be either external or internal. Internal style sheets define styles in the `<head>` section of an individual Web page, and the styles apply only to the page in which they're defined. External style sheets define styles in a text file saved with a .css extension. You can then link multiple pages to the style sheet. When you modify a style in an external style sheet, the change is reflected in every page linked to that style sheet.

Defining styles

The three most common CSS styles are described in the following table.

Style type	Description

Element styles	Element styles define the formatting of HTML elements. An element style overrides the default formatting for that HTML element. The syntax to define an element style is:
	
	`element { property: value; }`
	
	For example, an element style for the paragraph tag might be:
	
	`p { font-weight: bold; }`

Class styles	You can use class styles to create and name your own elements. For example, you can create a class of the `<p>` element named something like "important" that applies bold, red text. Any paragraphs that are given that class name appear with those styles. You can apply class styles to multiple elements on a page. The syntax for a class style is:
	
	`.className { property: value; }`
	
	The class name must begin with a period. For example, if you want to create the rule mentioned above, you would write:
	
	`.important { font-weight: bold; color: red; }`

ID styles	You can also use ID styles to create and name your own elements. However, although class styles can apply to multiple elements in a page, ID styles can be applied only to one element per page. ID styles are particularly useful for defining major content sections that appear only once in a page, such as a `<div>` element named "navigation" to define a navigation bar, or a `<div>` element named "footer" to define the page footer. The syntax for an ID style is:
	
	`#IDname { property: value; }`
	
	The ID name must begin with the number sign (#). For example:
	
	`#footer { font-size: 10px; color: gray; }`

When you define an element style, the effects are immediately apparent in any pages that contain that element and are linked to the style sheet. After you create class or ID styles, you need to apply them manually to the desired HTML elements.

You don't need to learn the details of CSS coding to start applying CSS styles to your Web pages. You can create the styles using by dialog boxes and task panes, and SharePoint Designer will write the necessary code for you.

Do it!

C-1: Discussing style sheets

Questions and answers

1. What is a style sheet?

2. What are the two main style sheet types?

3. What are the advantages of using an external style sheet?

4. When might you want to use an internal style sheet?

5. What is CSS?

6. Name three style types that you can define in a style sheet.

7. If you want all level-one headings in your site to appear in gray text, what type of style should you use?

8. Describe a scenario in which you would want to create a class style.

9. Describe a scenario in which you would want to create an ID style.

External style sheets

Explanation

There are several advantages to using external style sheets, including:

- They reduce the size of the Web site, because style definitions occur in only one place (rather than repeated on each Web page in the site). A smaller Web site downloads faster and is much easier to maintain.
- A designer can make changes across multiple pages by editing styles in one place. The designer doesn't have to open each HTML file to make style changes.
- Making changes to the single CSS style sheet saves time and avoids introducing errors or style inconsistency to the pages in the site.

To create an external style sheet:

1. Choose File, New to open the New dialog box. The Page tab is active by default.
2. In the General category, select CSS to specify that you want to create a CSS document.
3. Click OK.
4. Save the file with a .css extension. (To help with site organization, you might want to save the style sheet to a subfolder within the site.)

To link a page to an external style sheet:

1. Open the page to which you want to link the style sheet.
2. In the Manage Styles/Apply Styles pane, click Attach Style Sheet to open the Attach Style Sheet dialog box, shown in Exhibit 3-10.
3. In the URL box, enter the path to the style sheet, or click Browse to navigate to it.
4. Under Attach to, select whether you want to link the style sheet only to the current page, or to all pages in the site.
5. Under Attach as, verify that Link is selected.
6. Click OK to attach the style sheet.

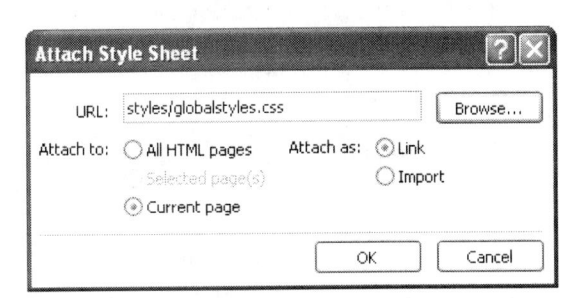

Exhibit 3-10: The Attach Style Sheet dialog box

Style sheets and templates

If you're using a template to maintain your site pages, you can link an external style sheet to the template document, instead of linking it to each individual page in the site. The styles attached to the template are automatically available to any pages linked to the template. This can save you a lot of time and effort.

Do it!

C-2: Creating and attaching an external style sheet

Here's how	Here's why
1 Choose **File, New...**	To open the New dialog box. The Page tab is active by default. You'll create an external style sheet.
2 In the left pane, verify that **General** is selected	
In the middle pane, double-click **CSS**	To create a new, blank CSS document.
3 Verify that Untitled_1.css is activated	SharePoint Designer created a new, blank style sheet with a default name.
4 Choose **File, Save**	The Save As dialog box appears.
Verify that the contents of the Outlander folder is displayed	(In the Save In box.) You'll save the style sheet in a new subfolder.
5 In the top-right corner of the dialog box, click	To create a new folder.
Type **styles**	To name the folder.
Press ← ENTER	images recipes aboutus.htm index.htm styles
6 Double-click the styles folder	To open it.
Edit the File name box to read **globalstyles.css**	External style sheets must be saved with a .css file extension.
Click **Save**	Next, you'll attach the style sheet to the template document.
7 Switch to the Outlander template	At the top of the work area, activate outlander.dwt.

8	Activate the Manage Styles pane	
	In the Manage Styles pane, click **Attach Style Sheet**	
		The Attach Style Sheet dialog box appears.
9	Click **Browse**	The Select Style Sheet File dialog box appears.
	Navigate to the styles folder, and select **globalstyles.css**	The styles folder is up one level, in the Outlander folder.
	Click **Open**	
		To attach the style sheet to the page. The URL box shows the path from the root site folder to the location of the style sheet.
10	Verify that Link is selected	
		You'll create a link to this style sheet, rather than embedding its styles directly in the page.
11	Click **OK**	To close the Attach External Style Sheet dialog box. The template looks the same, because no styles have been defined yet in the external style sheet. You'll verify that the style sheet is linked to the template.
12	In Code view, scroll to the top of the page	If necessary.
	In the Head section of the document, locate the link to the style sheet	
		(Around line 10.) The code now includes a link to globalstyles.css.
13	Switch to Design view	
14	Save the template	Click Yes and Close in the alert boxes to update any documents linked to the template.

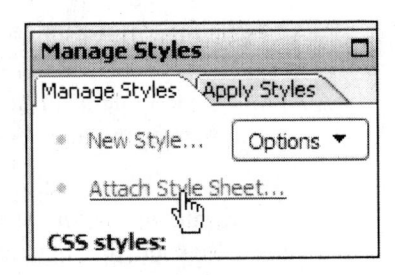

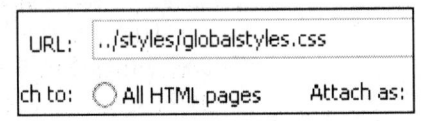

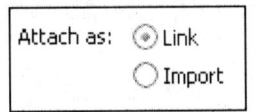

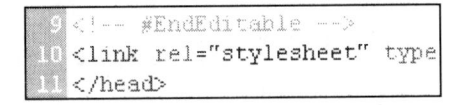

Element styles

Explanation

As you plan the design of your site, it's likely that you'll decide ahead of time on some stylistic aspects, such as fonts, colors, and images. Often, you can use CSS to implement some of these choices throughout a site, without having to apply styles to content on each page. You can do this by creating element styles.

An *element style* redefines the default formatting for HTML elements. For example, if you create an element style that makes all level-one headings blue, any pages linked to the style sheet automatically have blue level-one headings.

To create an element style in an external style sheet:

1. In the Manage Styles/Apply Styles pane, click New Style. The New Style dialog box appears, as shown in Exhibit 3-11.
2. In the Selector box, enter the tag you want to define, or select a tag from the drop-down list.
3. In the Define In list, select Existing style sheet.
4. Verify that the style sheet is visible in the URL box. If the style sheet wasn't open and active when you clicked New Style, you need to click Browse and navigate to the style sheet.
5. Use the formatting categories to set the desired formatting for the tag.
6. Click OK to close the dialog box and set the style.

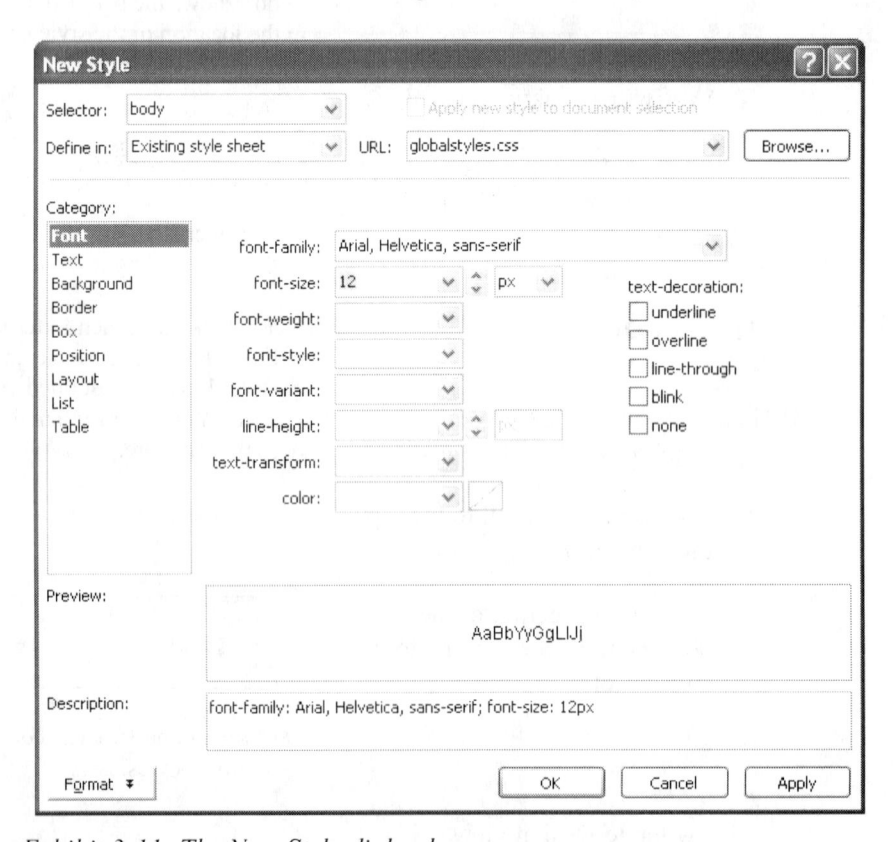

Exhibit 3-11: The New Style dialog box

CSS properties

Each CSS rule (each command that defines styles for various elements) may contain multiple properties. Each property is a formatting attribute, such as color, font face, and font size. SharePoint Designer organizes properties into several categories, as shown in the New Style dialog box in Exhibit 3-11. Each property has associated value options that you can apply.

Font sets

Applying font sets is a popular method of formatting text. A *font set* is a list of similar fonts. When you apply a font set, the user's Web browser attempts to display the text in the first font specified in the set. If the first font isn't available on the user's computer, it uses the second font in the set. If that font isn't available, it attempts to apply the third font in the set, and so on. A font set should end with a generic font specification, serif, sans-serif, or mono-spaced. This guarantees that, even if a user doesn't have any of the fonts listed in your font set, at least the general font type is displayed.

The difference between serif and sans-serif fonts is the style in which the letters are formed. A serif font has *flourishes* (decorations) at the ends of its characters, while sans-serif fonts don't, as illustrated in Exhibit 3-12. Mono-spaced fonts are font faces such as Courier and Courier New, in which each character takes up the same amount of horizontal space and resemble typewriter text.

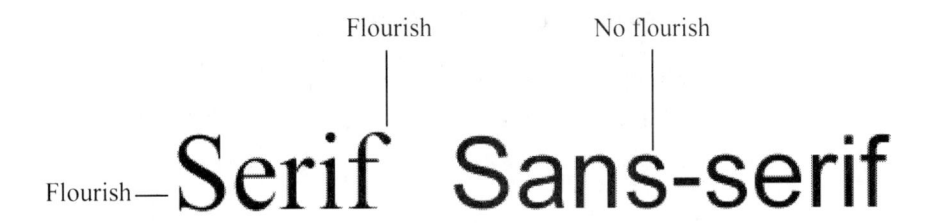

Exhibit 3-12: Serif and sans-serif fonts

Font size

There are many units of measurement that you can use to control font size. The most commonly used are points and pixels. A point is a unit of print measurement that doesn't translate well to the screen. Pixels are a more appropriate choice for display on a Web page. Using pixels typically produces the most consistent results across various browsers and platforms.

Do it!

C-3: Defining element styles

Here's how	Here's why
1 Switch to globalstyles.css	To view the blank style sheet. You'll define a style for the `<body>` tag, and create heading styles.
2 In the Manage Styles pane, click **New Style**	To open the New Style dialog box. By default, the Selector field is set to create a new class style (a period followed by the text newStyle1), but you can define element styles by selecting a tag from the drop-down list.
3 From the Selector list, select **body**	To create a CSS rule that defines the styles for the entire body section of a Web page. You want to define the style within the external style sheet (globalstyles.css), and not within the current page.
4 From the Define in list, select **Existing style sheet**	The URL box automatically selects the only style sheet in the site, which is globalstyles.css.
5 From the font-family list, select **Arial, Helvetica, sans-serif**	This is a font set of similar font faces, ending with a generic font face.
6 Click to place the insertion point in the font-size box, and type **12**	The font-size measurement type automatically selects px, which is an abbreviation for pixels.
7 Click **OK**	To close the dialog box. The code for the style is now visible in the style sheet.
8 Save the style sheet	You'll preview the results in the template.
9 Switch to aboutus.htm	(At the top of the Document window, activate aboutus.htm.) All the body text is now formatted as 12px, Arial, with the exception of the headings and subheadings, which remain a larger font size.
Observe the Manage Styles pane	The body element style now appears in the list. Next, you'll define new styles for the h1 and h2 headings.

10	In the Manage Styles pane, click **New Style**	To open the New Style dialog box. (You don't need to activate globalstyles.css to add styles to it.)
	From the Selector list, select **h1**	Scroll down.
	From the Define in list, select **Existing style sheet**	The About Us page is active, so you need to navigate to the globalstyles.css style sheet.
11	Click **Browse…**	
	Select **globalstyles.css** and click **Open**	
12	In the font-size box, enter **22**	To set the font size for level-one headings.
13	From the color list, select the dark green color swatch	
14	Click **OK**	The level-one headings in the About Us page are now 22 pixels and green.
15	Create a new element style for the level-two headings	In the Manage Styles pane, click New Style. From the Selector list, select h2. Create the style in the globalstyles.css style sheet.
	Set the font-size to 16 pixels	
	Click **OK**	The level-two heading is updated with the new style definition.
16	Save the document	When you update the About Us page, the Save Embedded Files dialog box appears, indicating that the linked style sheet also needs to be updated.
	Click **OK**	
17	Switch to globalstyles.css	
	Observe the code	There are now three rules in the style sheet; one for the body element, one for the h1 element, and one for the h2 element.

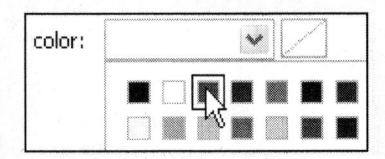

Class styles

Explanation

You can also create class styles, or "classes," to accompany HTML element styles—or to replace them. You can apply classes to any HTML element. For example, if you want to create a special type of paragraph that has styles different from normal paragraphs, you can create a class style. You can't achieve this by defining an element style for the `<p>` tag, because that would affect all paragraphs.

Class names must begin with a period, followed by the class name. Giving classes meaningful names can make site maintenance easier for both you and others who might work on the site in the future. For example, it would be easier to determine where and how a class style is used if it's named ".leadPara" instead of ".class2".

To create a class style:

1 In the Manage Styles/Apply Styles pane, click New Style. The New Style dialog box appears.
2 In the Selector box, enter a descriptive name for the style. Be sure to start the style name with a period.
3 In the Define In list, select Existing style sheet.
4 Verify that the style sheet is visible in the URL box. If the style sheet wasn't open and active when you clicked New Style, you need to click Browse and navigate to the style sheet.
5 Use the formatting categories to set the desired formatting for the class style.
6 Click OK to close the dialog box and set the style.

To apply a class style:

1 In Design view, select the content to which you want to apply the class style.
2 If the Manage Styles pane is active, activate Apply Styles to view the Apply Styles pane. A list of defined styles appears. Styles appear with the formatting they apply, as shown in Exhibit 3-13.
3 Click the class style you want to apply.

Exhibit 3-13: The Apply Styles pane

Text formatting   **3–27**

C-4: Creating and applying class styles

Do it!

Here's how	Here's why
1 In the Manage Styles pane, click **New Style**	
2 In the Selector box, type **emphasize**	SharePoint automatically includes the period. All class names must begin with a period.
From the Define in list, select **Existing style sheet**	
3 From the font-style list, select **italic**	
From the font-weight list, select **bold**	
Click **OK**	
4 Switch to aboutus.htm	
5 Scroll to the paragraph under "About our spices"	
Select **Every Outlander spice is of premium quality**	where the finished product must be consistent w el Every Outlander spice is of premium quality. Ou in retail stores.¶
6 In the Manage Styles pane, activate **Apply Styles**	
In the list, click **.emphasize**	The sentence within the paragraph is now bold and italicized.
7 Switch to Code view	
Observe the code that applies the class style	`<span class="emphasize">Every Outlander`
	SharePoint Designer defines the start and end of the style application by using a `<span>` tag, which is a generic inline container designed for applying styles such as this.
Switch to Design view	
8 Save and close all open files	When you update the About Us page, you need to update the globalstyles.css document at the same time.
9 Choose **File**, **Close Site**	To close the Outlander Web site.

Unit summary: Text formatting

Topic A In this topic, you learned how to import content into a Web page from an external document. You also converted **line breaks** into **paragraph breaks**, and you learned how to insert **non-breaking spaces** and **symbols**.

Topic B In this topic, you learned how to apply **structural tags** to text, and you created an **ordered list**, an **unordered list**, and a **nested list**.

Topic C In this topic, you created an **external style sheet** and linked a document to it. You also learned how to create **element styles**, and you created and applied **class styles**.

Independent practice activity

In this activity, you'll open an existing site and insert a copyright symbol in the site's template. Then, you'll format text by using element and class styles.

1. With the Open Site command, open the **Practice** folder (from the current unit folder).
2. Open **aboutus.htm**.
3. Open the outlander.dwt template, and replace the word "Copyright" in the copyright statement with a copyright symbol, similar to the example in Exhibit 3-14. (*Hint:* Remove the font formatting from the symbol before you import it.)
4. Return to the About Us page, and apply h1 formatting to the following three headings:
   - All Spiced Up!
   - About our spices
   - Expansion Project
5. Apply h2 formatting to the following four headings:
   - About our spice blends and sausage-making supplies
   - About our other products
   - About our bulk packages
   - The project team
6. Create a new external style sheet named **outlanderstyles.css**. Store the style sheet in a subfolder named **styles**.
7. Create a new element style for the `<body>` tag to format all the text in a document using the "Arial, Helvetica, sans-serif" font set. Set the font size to 12 pixels.
8. Save the style sheet and link it to the outlander.dwt template.
9. Save and close the template. (Also, save any pages linked to the template.)
10. Create new element styles for the `<h1>` and `<h2>` tags to format all the headings. Reduce the size of both heading tags, similar to the example shown in Exhibit 3-15. Select an orange color for the level-one headings.
11. Create two new class styles that apply styles of your choice. Give the class styles meaningful names, and be sure to start the class style names with a period.
12. In aboutus.htm, apply the class styles to the text of your choice.
13. Save and close all open documents, and close the site.

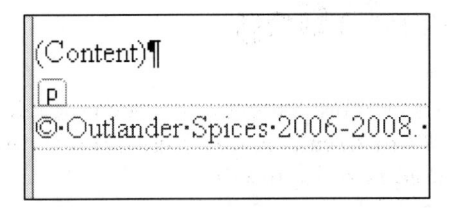

Exhibit 3-14: The template after step 3

Exhibit 3-15: The About Us page after step 10

Review questions

1 True or false? A line break forces text to begin on a new line but within the same paragraph.

2 Benefits of structuring your documents in a meaningful, logical hierarchy of elements include which of the following items? (Select all that apply.)

   A Helps to establish consistency on your pages

   B Saves you time and effort when you later update your pages

   C Allows your pages to be indexed by search engines more efficiently

   D Improves the appearance of your Web pages when viewed in a browser

   E Allows SharePoint Designer to function optimally

3 A font that has flourishes (decorations) at the ends of its characters is:

   A a serif font.

   B a sans-serif font.

   C a mono-spaced font.

   D plain text.

4 Why are font faces best specified in *font sets*?

5 When you have a list of items that follow a particular sequence, you should format them as a(n):

   A unordered list.

   B ordered list.

   C nested list.

   D definition list.

6 If you want all the level-two headings in your site to have the same styles, you should:

   A create an internal element style for the h2 tag.

   B create an external element style for the h2 tag.

   C create an internal class style.

   D create an external class style.

7 If you want to create a special type of paragraph with extra large text, and you think you'll use it several times throughout your site, it's best to:

   A create an internal element style for the p tag.

   B create an external element style for the p tag.

   C create an external class style and apply it to the relevant paragraphs.

   D create an external ID style and apply it to the relevant paragraphs.

Unit 4
Web page layout

Unit time: 45 minutes

Complete this unit, and you'll know how to:

A Create content sections by using <div> tags, and create and apply ID styles.

B Create fixed and fluid layouts; apply margins, padding, and borders; and apply the float and clear properties.

Topic A: Basic CSS layout

Explanation

You can precisely control the positioning and formatting of your page elements by creating and applying CSS styles. Using CSS for page layout is faster, more efficient, and more flexible than using large, table-based layouts, especially if you use the same layout for multiple pages. By placing the layout rules in an external style sheet, you can link an unlimited number of pages to the style sheet to control the layout and other styles from a single location. Any changes you make to the style sheet appear universally throughout the site. CSS also helps reduce the amount of code required to design a Web site, because most, if not all, of the style rules are stored in the style sheet rather than repeated in every page.

Page structure and layout

Most Web pages are divided into sections, as illustrated in Exhibit 4-1. For example, many Web pages have a banner or a navigation bar at the top of the page and perhaps several columns of information.

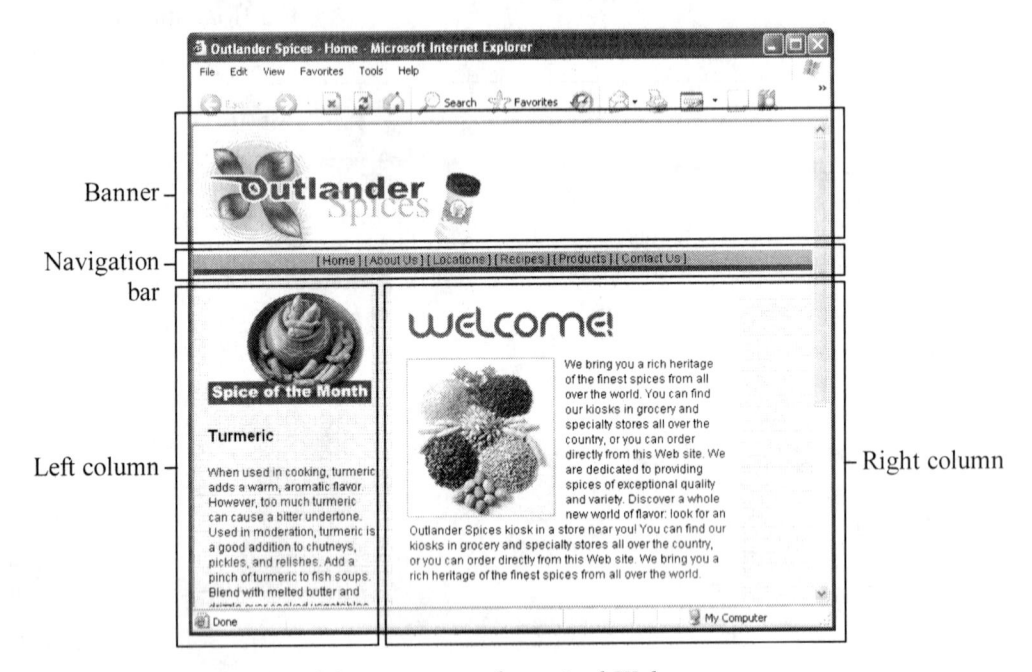

Exhibit 4-1: An example of the structure of a typical Web page

The <div> tag

You can use the `<div>` ("division") tag to define document sections. The `<div>` tag is a generic HTML element that acts as a container for page elements. For example, each section shown in Exhibit 4-1 is defined by a `<div>`, and each `<div>` is given an ID. Each ID uniquely identifies and names each section and enables you to apply styles to an entire section and every element contained within it.

Exhibit 4-2 shows the code used to define a column of content on a page. All the page elements included in the column are nested inside the `<div>` tag, which has the ID "leftcolumn." You can target CSS styles to this ID, so that the entire section is formatted with those styles.

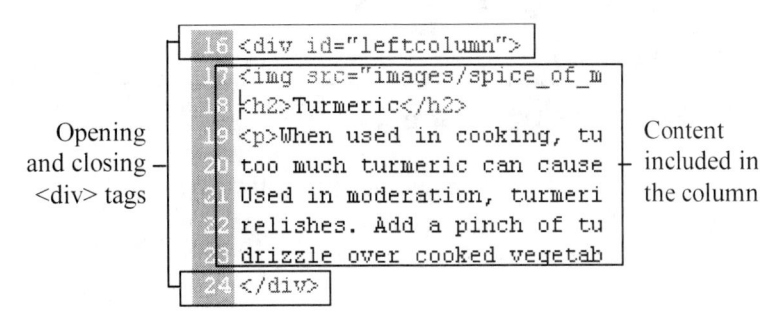

```
16 <div id="leftcolumn">
17 <img src="images/spice_of_m
18 <h2>Turmeric</h2>
19 <p>When used in cooking, tu
20 too much turmeric can cause
21 Used in moderation, turmeri
22 relishes. Add a pinch of tu
23 drizzle over cooked vegetab
24 </div>
```

Opening and closing `<div>` tags — lines 16 and 24.
Content included in the column — lines 17–23.

Exhibit 4-2: An example of content section defined by a <div> tag

To define a content section by using a `<div>` tag to contain existing content:

1. Select the content that you want to establish as a distinct section. You can use the Quick Tag Selector to help make the selection.
2. In the Toolbox pane, under Tags, right-click the `<div>` tag option.
3. From the drop-down list, select Wrap. This wraps the selected content into a `<div>` section.

Do it!

A-1: Defining content sections

Here's how	Here's why
1 Choose **File, Open Site...**	
Navigate to the current unit folder	If necessary.
Open the Outlander site	The folders and pages in the site appear in the Folder pane and in the work area.
2 Open the Outlander template	(Expand the templates subfolder, and double-click outlander.dwt.) The template contains a logo, some navigation text, and a copyright statement. You'll use `<div>` tags to organize the page into sections. Later, you'll use CSS to format the sections to control the overall layout.
3 At the top of the page, click the logo image	To select it.
4 In the Toolbox pane, under Tags, right-click **`<div>`**	A drop-down list appears.
Select **Wrap**	SharePoint Designer wraps the image in a `<div>` container. Later, you'll assign an ID to this container.
5 Triple-click any of the text in the navigation bar	To select the entire paragraph.
6 In the Toolbox pane, right-click **`<div>`** and select **Wrap**	Again, SharePoint Designer wraps the selected content within a `<div>` container.
7 Wrap the copyright statement in another `<div>` section	Triple-click the copyright statement to select it. In the Toolbox pane, right-click `<div>` and select Wrap.
8 Save the template	
Click **Yes**	To update the pages linked to the template.
Click **Close**	

ID styles

Explanation

After you've established content sections by dividing the page into separate `<div>` containers, you can use ID styles to position and format each section. ID style names must begin with a number sign (#), followed by an appropriate name that identifies the section, such as #navigation or #footer.

When you defined `<div>` sections in the preceding activity, SharePoint Designer assigned default ID names to each section. You can choose to leave those default names until you're ready to apply ID styles to those sections, or you can rename the IDs as soon as you create the `<div>` section.

To create an ID style:

1. In the Manage Styles/Apply Styles pane, click New Style. The New Style dialog box appears.
2. In the Selector box, enter a descriptive name for the style. Be sure to start the style name with a number sign (#).
3. In the Define In list, select Existing style sheet.
4. Verify that the style sheet is visible in the URL box. If the style sheet wasn't open and active when you clicked New Style, you need to click Browse and navigate to the style sheet.
5. Using the formatting categories, apply the desired styles.
6. Click OK.

Do it!

A-2: Creating ID styles

Here's how	Here's why
1 From the styles subfolder, open **globalstyles.css**	(In the Folder List pane, expand the styles folder, and double-click globalstyles.css.) You'll create ID styles to format and control the layout for the page. These styles will be applied to the `<div>` tags you created earlier.
2 In the Apply Styles pane, click **New Style**	To open the New Style dialog box. ID styles always begin with a # sign.
3 In the Selector box, edit the default text to read **#logo**	
From the Define in list, select **Existing style sheet**	You'll create a white background for the logo section.

4	From the Category list, select **Background**	The right pane changes to show background style options.
	From the background-color list, select the white color swatch	
		The white background will stretch across the full width of a browser window.
	Click **OK**	To close the dialog box and create the style. Next, you'll create a style for the navigation bar.
5	In the Apply Styles pane, click **New Style**	To open the New Style dialog box.
6	In the Selector box, edit the default text to read **#navbar**	
	From the Define in list, select **Existing style sheet**	You'll use a light green background for the navigation bar.
7	From the Category list, select **Background**	The right pane changes to show background options for the style.
	From the background-color list, select **More Colors…**	
		To open the More Colors dialog box.
	Select the green color with the value **Hex = {99,CC,00}** and click **OK**	
		The Preview pane shows the selected background color. You'll also create a thick dark green border along the bottom.

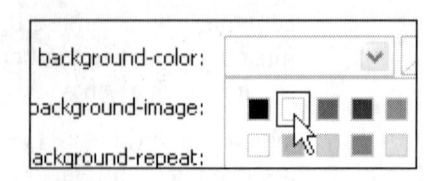

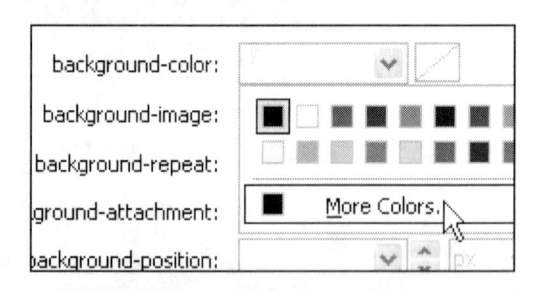

8 From the Category list, select
Border

Below border-style, clear
Same for all

From the bottom list, select **solid**

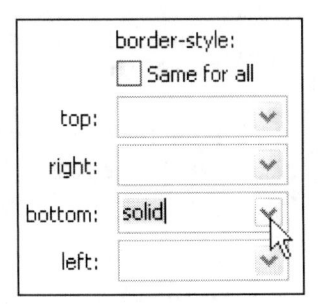

9 Below border-width, clear
Same for all

From the bottom list, select **thick** — The Preview pane shows a thick black border along the bottom of the content.

10 Below border-color, clear **Same for all**

Select the Green color swatch for the bottom border

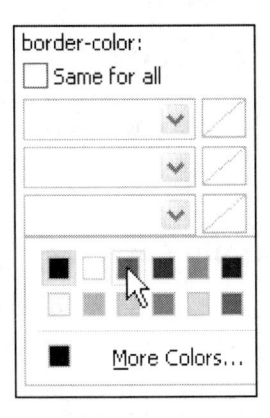

To change the black bottom border to green.

Click **OK** — To close the dialog box and create the style. The style options you selected are listed in the style sheet. Lastly, you'll create a style for the copyright statement.

11	In the Apply Styles pane, click **New Style**	To open the New Style dialog box.
	In the Selector box, edit the default text to read **#copyright**	
	From the Define in list, select **Existing style sheet**	
12	From the Category list, verify that **Font** is selected	You'll set the font size for the copyright statement to be bold but smaller than the rest of the text on the page.
	From the font-size list, select **smaller**	
	From the font-weight list, select **bold**	
13	From the Category list, select **Block**	
	From the text-align list, select **center**	To center the copyright statement.
14	Click **OK**	To close the dialog box and create the style.
15	Save the style sheet	

Apply ID styles

Explanation

Like class styles, you can apply an ID style to any page element. However, unlike class styles, ID styles must be unique. They may appear only once per document.

To apply an ID style:

1 In Design view, select the `<div>` section to which you want to apply the style. To do this, you can click inside the section, and then use the Quick Tag Selector to select the `<div>`.
2 If the Manage Styles pane is active, activate Apply Styles to view the Apply Styles pane.
3 In the pane, click the ID style you want to apply.

Do it!

A-3: Applying ID styles

Here's how	Here's why
1 Switch to outlander.dwt	You'll apply the new styles to the logo, navigation bar, and copyright sections.
2 Click the logo image	To select it.
3 In the Quick Tag Selector, click **<div>**	To select the `<div>` that contains the image.
4 In the Apply Styles pane, click **#logo**	To apply the ID style to the selected content.
Observe the Quick Tag Selector	The div appears with its ID.
Click another area of the page	To deselect the logo. You applied a white background to this section, and it stretches across the entire width of the page.
5 Click in the navigation bar	To place the insertion point.
6 In the Quick Tag Selector, click **<div >**	To select the `<div>` tag that contains the navigation bar text.
7 In the Apply Styles pane, click **#navbar**	To apply this ID style to the navigation bar section.
8 Click anywhere on the page	To deselect the copyright section.
Apply the #copyright style to the copyright statement	Using the Quick Tag Selector, select the `<div>` that contains the copyright statement, and then click #copyright in the Apply Styles pane.
9 Save and close the template	Click Yes and Close in the alert boxes to update any documents linked to the template.

Topic B: Basic layout techniques

Explanation

Most Web page layouts are based on either a fixed or a flexible width. In a fixed-width layout, the width of the page content remains the same, no matter how large or small a user's monitor or browser window might be. In a flexible, or "fluid" layout, the width of the container that holds the page content is sized relative to the size of the browser window.

Fixed layouts vs. fluid layouts

When you're planning your site design, keep in mind that, when it comes to a fixed-width layout versus a fluid layout, one design option isn't necessarily better than the other, and they both have their places. However, fluid layouts can help ensure that your page layout is optimized for each user that visits your site. Users come to a site with a wide variety of monitor sizes and browser window size preferences. A fluid layout can prevent large gaps of empty space for users who prefer a large browser window, as illustrated in Exhibit 4-3.

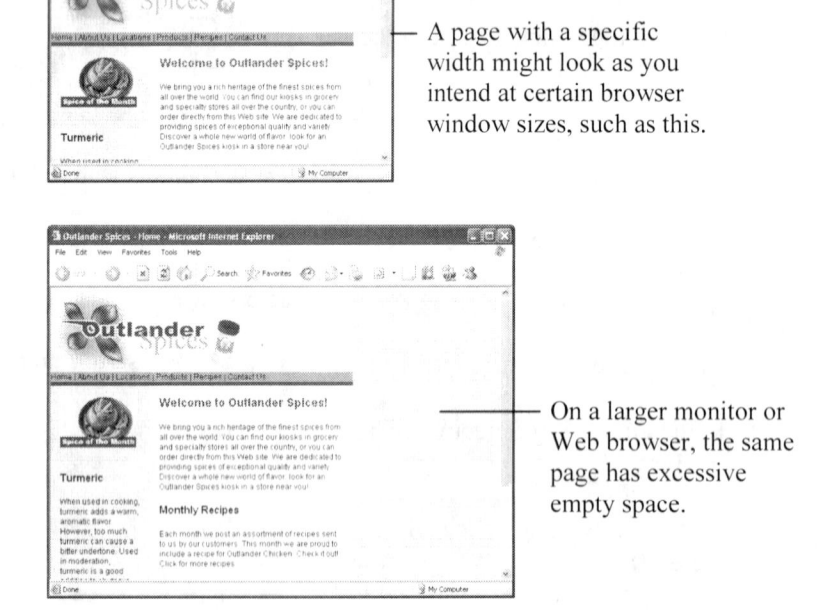

— A page with a specific width might look as you intend at certain browser window sizes, such as this.

— On a larger monitor or Web browser, the same page has excessive empty space.

Exhibit 4-3: Examples of a fixed-width layout

On the other hand, using a flexible layout can result in long lines of text in larger browsers, which might not be desirable. Using a fixed layout gives the designer full control over the appearance of the layout, while a fluid layout allows each user to determine the overall width of the layout.

Block elements and inline elements

Block elements are those HTML elements that create a line break, such as the `<p>` tag, `<div>`, headings, and many other elements. *Inline elements* don't create line breaks but are used within lines of text instead. Inline elements include the `<span>` tag, `<b>`, `<em>`, and many other elements that are typically used to define specific words or phrases rather than entire blocks of content.

Creating a fixed width layout

To create a fixed-width layout, you need to apply a width value (in pixels or another absolute value) to your content sections or to an outer wrapper that contains your entire page layout. You can't use a relative unit of measurement, such as percentages. To apply a width to an element, open the New Style dialog box, or the Modify Style dialog box. From the Category list, select Position, and then enter a value in the width box.

Creating a fluid layout

By default, every block element has a width of 100% of its parent element. In many layout scenarios, the `<body>` element is the parent element for a series of `<div>` tags that define the major content sections. Therefore, if you don't specify a fixed width for an outer layout container or the individual page sections within your layout, they automatically resize according to the size of the browser window.

If you don't want the content to abut the edges of the browser window, you can also specify a percentage width that isn't quite the full width of the browser window, such as a value of 95%.

Do it!

B-1: Creating fixed and fluid layouts

Here's how	Here's why
1 Open aboutus.htm	(In the Folder List pane, double-click aboutus.htm). The page content spans the full width of the window, which is the default behavior of an element that does not have a fixed width.
2 Place the insertion point anywhere in the editable text	
Press CTRL + A	To select all the editable text.
3 Wrap the selection in a `<div>` tag	In the Toolbox pane, right-click `<div>` and select Wrap.
4 In the Apply Styles pane, click **New Style**	To open the New Style dialog box.
Edit the Selector box to read **#mainContent**	
From the Define in list, select **Existing style sheet**	
Link the globalstyles style sheet	Click Browse and navigate to the location of the style sheet.
5 Check **Apply new style to document selection**	☑ Apply new style to document selection URL: styles/globalstyles.css To apply the style automatically to the selected content.
6 From the Category list, select **Background**	
From the background-color list, select the white color swatch	
Click **OK**	
7 Save the page	
Click **OK**	To update the globalstyles style sheet.
Preview the page in Internet Explorer	The outer container "#mainContent" appears with a white background.
Resize the browser window	As you resize the window, the text reflows. The container doesn't have a fixed-width setting applied to it, so it's fluid by default.

Web page layout

8 Close the browser

9 In the Manage Styles pane, right-click **#mainContent**

   Choose **Modify Style...**

10 From the Category list, select **Position** — You'll format the page content so that it spans a percentage of the browser window. You'll also make the background behind the text white.

   In the width box, enter **550** — Pixels are the default unit of measurement. You can use pixels to create fixed-width elements and layouts.

   Click **OK** — To close the Modify Style dialog box.

11 Save the page

   Click **OK** — To update the globalstyles style sheet.

   Preview the page in Internet Explorer

   Resize the browser window — The #mainContent section doesn't reflow, no matter how large or small the browser window is set. This is a simple example of a fixed layout.

   Close the browser

12 In the Manage Styles pane, right-click **#mainContent**

   Choose **Modify Style...**

   From the Category list, select **Position**

   Specify a width of 95%, as shown

   width: 95 %

   Click **OK**

13 Save the page

   Click **OK** — To update the globalstyles style sheet.

   Preview the page in Internet Explorer

   Resize the browser window — The #mainContent section is always 95% of the width of the browser window, and the text inside the element reflows to fit the available size. This is a simple example of a fluid layout.

   Close the browser

Margins, padding, and borders

Explanation

An element's *margin* is the space between it and other elements; *padding* is the space between an element's content and its border. In Exhibit 4-4, the element's padding is the space between its content (text or image) and the solid black border. The space between the border and the dotted line represents the element's margin.

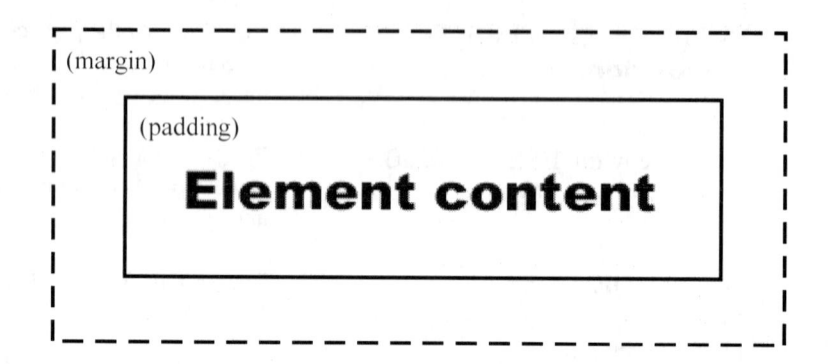

Exhibit 4-4: Margins and padding

If you want to increase the space between adjacent elements, applying margins is typically the best option. If you want to increase the space between an element's content and its borders, you need to use padding. To apply margins and padding, open the New Style dialog box. From the Category list, select Box. If you want to apply the same values to all four sides of an element, be it a margin or padding, verify that Same for all is checked. If you want to apply different values, clear Same for all.

For example, if you want to apply a margin value to the top of an element, clear Same for all, and then enter a value in the top box.

Borders

You can achieve a variety of different design effects with borders. You can give any rendered element a border, on all four sides or on individual sides. An element's border is drawn around its outermost edge, between its padding and its margin, as shown in Exhibit 4-5.

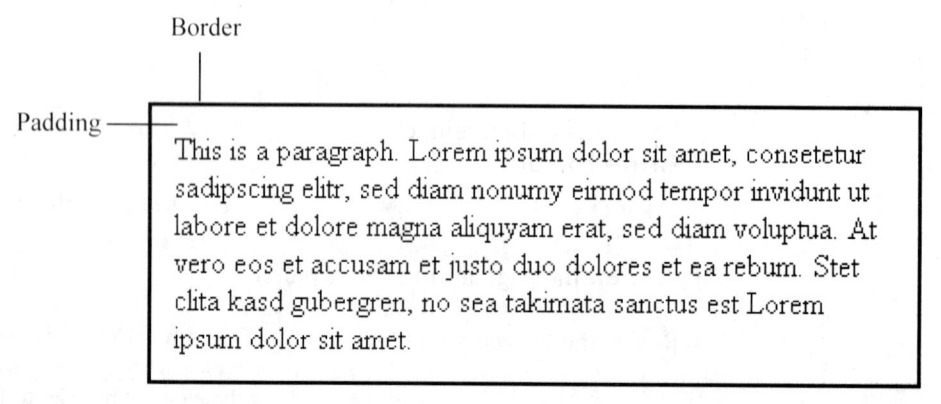

Exhibit 4-5: A solid border around a paragraph that has padding applied to it

Borders are a popular design tool, because they can draw the user's eye to an element and provide a way to separate and emphasize content sections visually.

Border styles

There are eight predefined border styles that you can apply to an element, as shown in Exhibit 4-6. These border styles vary slightly, depending on the width of the border and the browser in use.

Solid	Groove
Double	Ridge
Dotted	Inset
Dashed	Outset

Exhibit 4-6: Border styles

You can apply borders by using the New Style dialog box or the Modify Style dialog box. In either dialog box, select Border from the Category list. Under border-style, border-width, and border-color, apply the desired settings. If you want to apply various border values to individual sides of an element, clear Same for all.

Do it!

B-2: Applying margins, padding, and borders

Here's how	Here's why
1 In the Manage Styles pane, right-click **#mainContent**	
Choose **Modify Style...**	
2 From the Category list, select **Position**	
From the width list, select **auto**	To reset the default width, which is the same as having no width setting.
3 From the Category list, select **Box**	
To the right of margin, clear **Same for all**	You'll apply a left and right margin to the main content section.
Set the left and right margin to 5%	margin: ☐ Same for all top: 0 px right: 5 % bottom: 0 px left: 5 %
Click **OK**	To close the Modify Style dialog box.

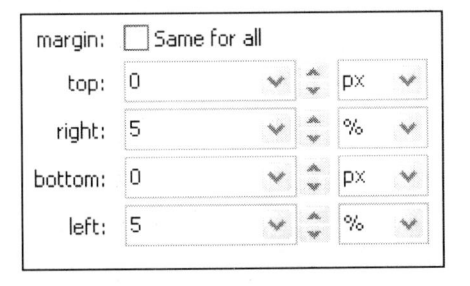

4 Save the page

Click **OK**	To update the globalstyles style sheet.
Preview the page in Internet Explorer	The #mainContent section has a 5% margin on its left and right sides, so it's always set apart from the edge of the browser window, giving it the appearance of being centered on the page.
Resize the browser window	The content in the #mainContent section reflows to fit the available size, and the container always appears centered on the page.
Close the browser	

5 In the Manage Styles pane, right-click **#mainContent**

   Choose **Modify Style...**

6 From the Category list, select **Border**

Under border-style, from the top list, select **ridge**	A preview appears at the bottom of the dialog box.
Under border-width, clear **Same for all**	
Set the top border to 0, and all other sides to 3, as shown	border-width: ☐ Same for all 0 px 3 px 3 px 3 px
	You'll apply a border on three sides, excluding the top.

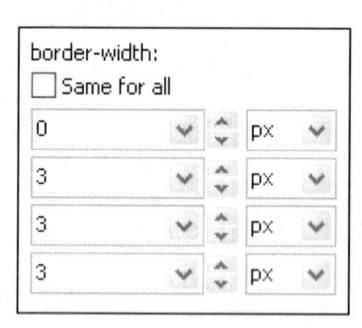

7 Under border-color, from the top list, select the dark green swatch

   Click **OK**

8 Save the page and update the style sheet

   Preview the page in Internet Explorer | The #mainContent section now has a green, 3-pixel ridge border around three sides. The content abuts the edges of the border. You'll improve the appearance and readability of the text by applying padding to this content section, which will add space between the content and the border.

   Close the browser

9 In the Manage Styles pane, right-click **#mainContent**

   Choose **Modify Style…**

10 From the Category list, select **Box**

   Under padding, in the top box, enter **15** | To apply 15 pixels of padding to all four sides of the container.

   Click **OK**

11 Save the page and update the style sheet

   Preview the page in Internet Explorer | The #mainContent section now has 15 pixels of padding on all four sides, creating space between the content and the border. It might appear that there's more padding at the top, but that's just because the level-one heading at the top creates some additional space above it.

   Close the browser

12 Close aboutus.htm

Multi-column layouts

Explanation

Two- and three-column layouts are popular on the Web. By default, elements are displayed, one on top of the other, in vertical succession. For example, in Exhibit 4-7, the content within one `<div>` container is displayed above the content in the next `<div>` container. One way to create a multi-column layout is to *float* one container to the left, so that the elements that follow it wrap to its right side.

Floating a container is a way of removing it from the normal flow of HTML elements. You can float an element (or container of elements) to either the left or right, which forces adjacent content to flow around it on the opposite side.

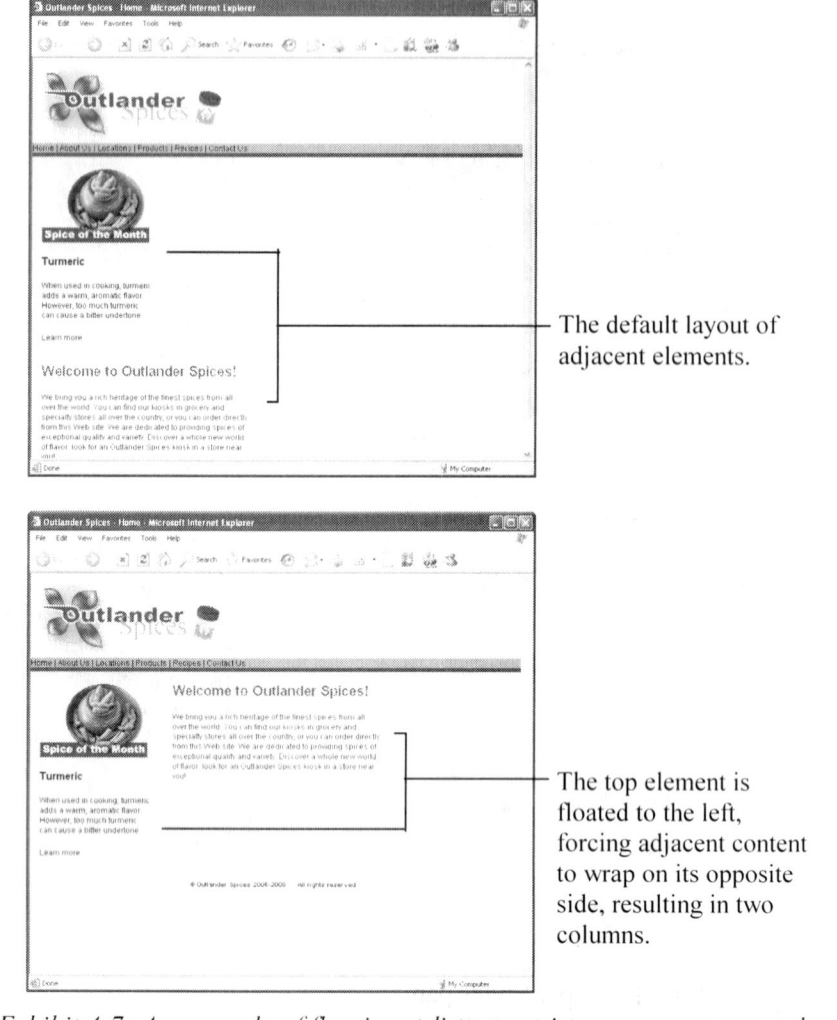

Exhibit 4-7: An example of floating <div> containers to create two columns

Duplicating styles

Some of your styles will be similar to others, with perhaps minor adjustments, depending on the content. Instead of creating a new style for each element, you can duplicate an existing style, and then make the adjustments to it for the element you're working on. To duplicate a style, in the Manage/Apply Styles pane, right-click the style you want to duplicate, and choose New Style Copy to open the New Style dialog box. The formatting options that were set for the original style are still active; you need only to change the style name (in the Selector box) and make any necessary adjustments for the new style.

Web page layout **4–19**

Do it! **B-3: Creating a two-column layout**

Here's how	Here's why
1 Open index.htm	
2 In the Apply Styles pane, click **New Style**	To open the New Style dialog box.
Edit the Selector box to read **#leftCol**	To create an ID style named leftCol.
From the Define in list, select **Existing style sheet**	To create two columns, you'll float one of the containers on the left side of the page.
Link the globalstyles style sheet	Click Browse and navigate to the globalstyles.css style sheet.
3 From the Category list, select **Layout**	
From the float list, select **left**	display: float: left clear:
4 From the Category list, select **Position**	
In the width box, enter **175**	When you want to create a multi-column layout, you need to establish width values for the sections that define the columns. By default, the unit of measure is set to pixels.
5 From the Category list, select **Box**	
Under padding, in the top box, enter **15**	
6 Click **OK**	
7 In the Apply Styles pane, right-click **#leftCol**	
Choose **New Style Copy…**	To open the New Style dialog box. Notice that, in the Category list, Box, Position, and Layout are all bold. This indicates that styles exist in those categories. (All the styles in the #leftCol style are active to prevent having to duplicate any styles.)
8 Edit the Selector box to read **#rightCol**	You'll adjust the style for the right column content.

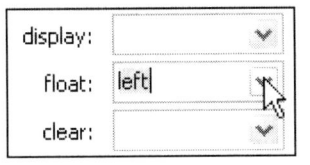

9	Select the Layout category	
	Delete the value in the float box	Select the value and press Delete.
10	Select the Position category	
	Change the width to **500**	To make the right column 550 pixels wide.
11	Select the Background category	
	From the background-color list, select the white swatch	To give the right column section a white background.
12	Click **OK**	To accept the changes. Now you'll apply the styles to the `<div>` sections.
13	Click the Spice of the Month image	To select it.
	In the Quick Tag Selector, click **<div>**	
		To select the `<div>` section that contains the image.
	In the Apply Styles pane, click **#leftCol**	The content section is confined to a container 175 pixels wide. Because it's floated to the left, adjacent content flows to its right. Next, you'll format the right column.
14	Click anywhere within the Welcome text	In the right column.
	In the Quick Tag Selector, click **<div>**	To select the `<div>` section that contains the bulk of the page content.
	In the Apply Styles pane, click **#rightCol**	The content changes to show a white background, and the #rightCol section is displayed to the right of the #leftCol section, creating a two-column layout. If it does not appear to the right in Design view, it's because the document window isn't wide enough.
15	Save the document and update the style sheet	
	Preview the page in Internet Explorer	The two-column layout appears as expected.

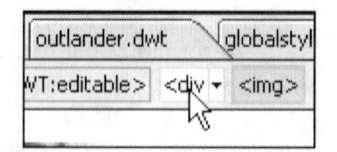

Clearing a floated element

Explanation

Sometimes there might be an element, such as a `<div>` container, that you don't want to wrap around a floated element. For example, as shown in Exhibit 4-8, the copyright statement wraps to the right of the left-floated container. However, you probably want the copyright statement to remain centered at the bottom of the page. If there were enough content in the page to span the full area of the left-floated element, this wouldn't be an issue. But when you're working with floated elements, you often find that there are some content sections that you don't want to wrap around a floated element. In such cases, you can *clear* the element.

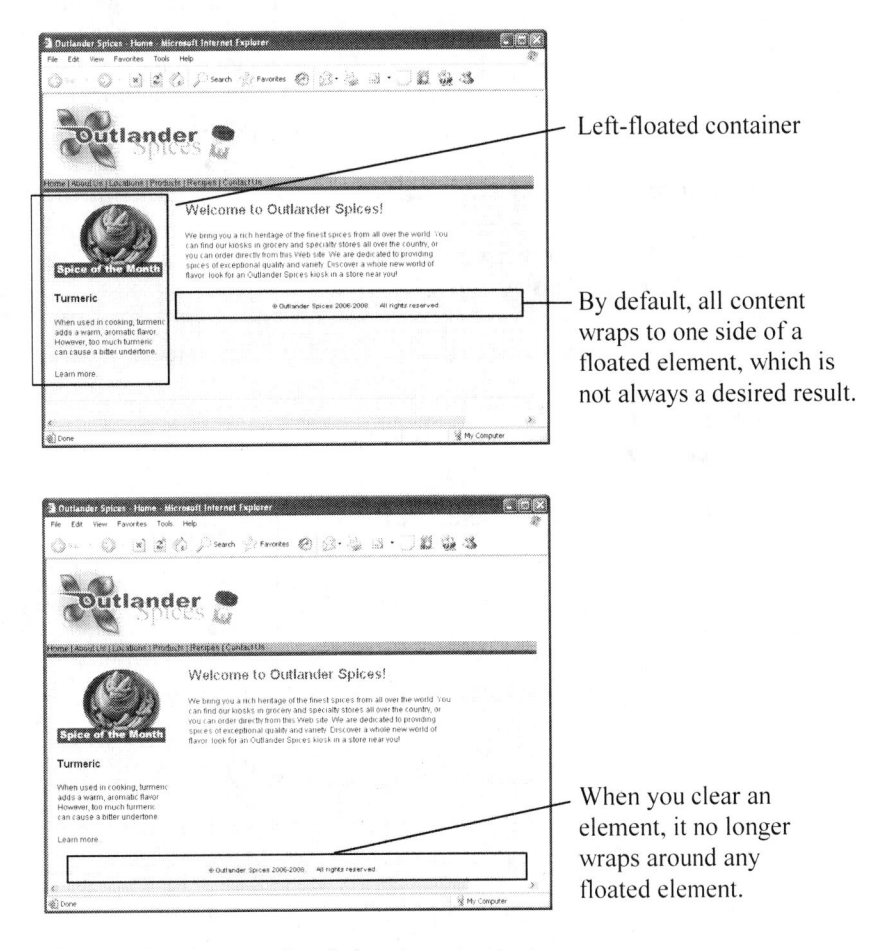

Exhibit 4-8: An example of clearing a container

To clear a floated element, open the New Style or Modify Style dialog box, depending on the circumstances. From the Category list, select Layout.

Do it!

B-4: Clearing a container

Here's how	Here's why
1 Maximize the browser window so that it fills the screen.	If necessary.
2 Observe the copyright statement	The copyright statement appears misaligned, because it wraps around the left-floated column along with the content in the right column. In this case, this is an undesired result. You want the copyright statement to remain centered at the bottom of the page, independent of either column. You'll fix this by clearing the copyright statement.
3 Close the browser	
4 In the Apply Styles pane, right-click **#copyright**	
Choose **Modify Style…**	To open the Modify Style dialog box.
5 From the Category list, select **Layout**	
6 From the clear list, select **left**	float: clear: left cursor:
	This tells the browser not to allow any content on its left side, which forces the copyright statement onto its own line, beneath the other content.
7 Click **OK**	
8 Save the page	
Click **OK**	To update the style sheet.
9 Preview the page in Internet Explorer	The copyright statement no longer follows the float command and is centered at the bottom of the page.
Close the browser	
10 Save and close all open files	
11 Choose **File**, **Close Site**	To close the Outlander Web site.

Web page layout **4–23**

Unit summary: Web page layout

Topic A In this topic, you defined **content sections** by wrapping content in **<div>** tags. You also created and applied **ID styles** to <div> containers.

Topic B In this topic, you learned basic layout techniques. You learned the difference between **fixed** and **fluid layouts**, and you applied **margins**, **padding**, and **borders** to an element. Then you created a **two-column layout** by **floating** an element, and you learned how to **clear** an element to prevent it from wrapping around a floated section.

Independent practice activity

In this activity, you'll define content sections and apply ID styles to them. You'll also create a fluid, two-column layout.

1 Open the Practice site (from the current unit folder).

2 Open **outlander.dwt** from the templates subfolder.

3 Select the logo image and wrap it in a <div> tag. (If the <div> tag is inserted below the image, drag the image into the <div> container.)

4 Click inside the navigation bar text and wrap it in a <div> tag.

5 Click inside the copyright statement and wrap it in a <div> tag.

6 Create a new ID style for the logo section. Name it **#logo** and save it in the existing style sheet, **outlanderstyles.css**. Give it a black background to match the black background of the image. (*Hint*: In the Manage Styles pane, click New Style....)

7 Apply the style to the logo div container. (*Hint:* Use the Quick Tag Selector to select the <div> that contains the image.)

8 Create a new ID style for the navigation bar named **#navbar**. Give the container a light orange background and a solid, thick, dark orange top border. Make the text bold.

9 Apply the #navbar style to the navigation bar <div> container.

10 Create a new ID style for the copyright statement named **#copyright**. Make the text in this container smaller, and centered on the page. (*Hint*: For alignment, use the Block category.)

11 Apply the style to the copyright text container. The page should look similar to the example shown in Exhibit 4-9.

12 Save and close the template. (Update the pages linked to the template.)

13 Open **index.htm**. (This page uses the template file you just modified.)

14 Create a new ID style named **#spiceMonth** for the "Spice of the Month" section. (The content is already wrapped in a <div>.) Define it in the existing style sheet **outlanderstyles.css**. Make this section a separate column on the left side of the page. The column should be about 175 pixels wide. Add a little padding to keep the content from the edges of its container. Finally, give it a **right margin** of 20 pixels.

15 Apply the style to the "Spice of the Month" section. (*Hint:* Use the Quick Tag Selector to select the <div> tag that contains the content for this section.)

16 Create a new ID style named **#content** for the Welcome text container. Give it a width of 500 pixels and a **top margin** of 40 pixels.

17 Apply the style to the Welcome text container. The page should look similar to the example shown in Exhibit 4-10.

18 Preview the page in Internet Explorer and then close the browser.

19 Save and close all open files.

20 Close the site.

Exhibit 4-9: The template after step 11

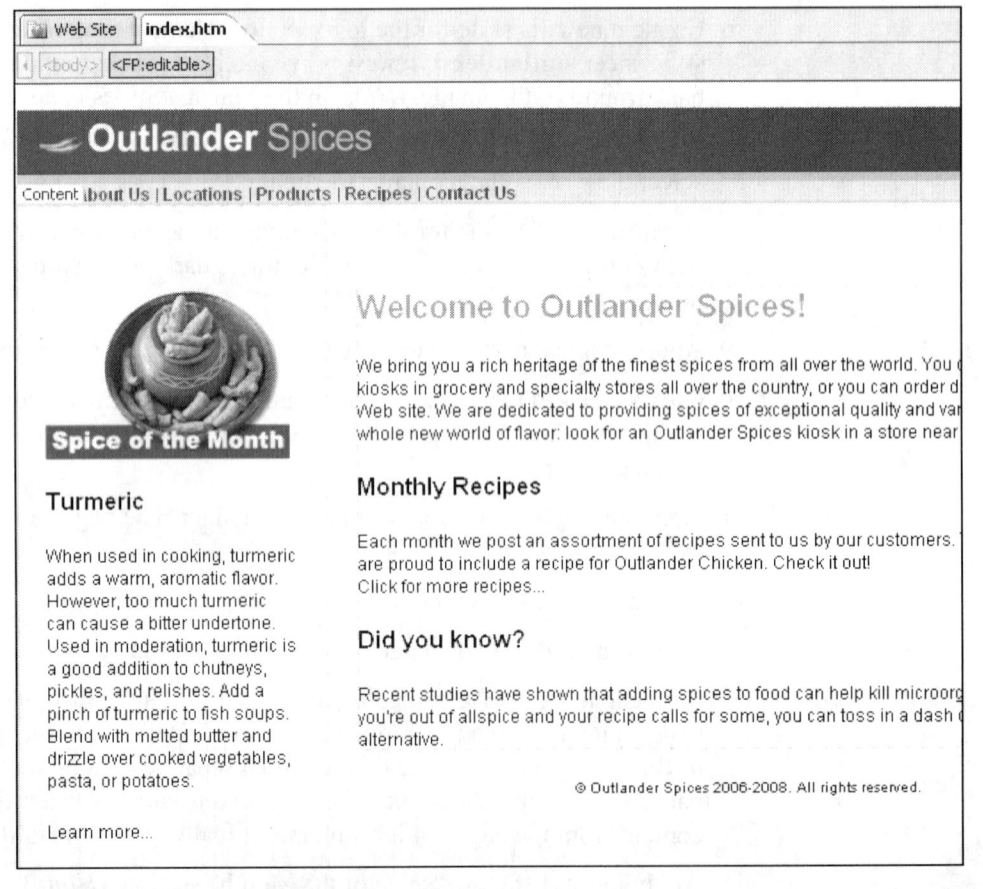

Exhibit 4-10: The home page after step 17

Review questions

1 Content sections are usually best defined by using

   A <p> tags and ID styles.

   B <div> tags and ID styles.

   C <div> tags and element styles.

   D <p> tags and element styles.

2 When you want to create a new style, but you want to apply many of the same styles that already appear in an existing style, you can:

   A Right-click the existing style, choose New Style Copy, and then make the desired modifications to the new style.

   B Copy and paste the style.

   C Use an inline style.

   D Right-click the existing style, choose Duplicate Style, and then make the desired modifications to the new style.

3 How do you apply a style to a <div> container?

   A Click to select an element on the page, and click the style in the Apply Styles pane.

   B Click to select an element on the page, and use the Quick Tag Selector to select the opening and closing <span> tags surrounding the content. Then click the style in the Apply Styles pane.

   C Drag to select all the page elements in the container, and click the style in the Apply Styles pane.

   D Click to select an element on the page, and use the Quick Tag Selector to select the <div> tag that contains it. Then click the style in the Apply Styles pane.

4 What's the difference between margins and padding?

5 What's the difference between block elements and inline elements?

6 True or false? When you *clear* a container, it removes the content from the container.

Unit 5
Images

Unit time: 40 minutes

Complete this unit, and you'll know how to:

A Identify the differences between image file formats, and apply image attributes and alternate text.

B Arrange images relative to adjacent text, and apply CSS margins and borders.

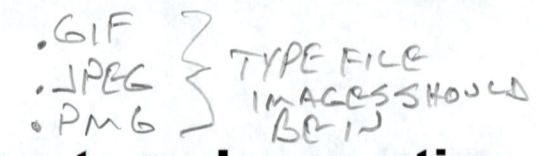

Topic A: Image formats and properties

Explanation

Images are an integral part of Web design. They catch the user's eye, they can introduce a unique artistic aspect to your design, and they deliver information in a way that text can't.

Images on the Web

File size is a vital consideration when using images on your Web pages. Large image files can take a long time to load in a user's browser. Try to keep your image file sizes as small as possible without sacrificing quality.

You can find images for your Web site from a variety of sources, including:

- Web sites that offer free images for downloading. Make sure that you read the Web site's downloading policy before you use any free images. Unauthorized use of images usually qualifies as copyright infringement.
- You can purchase image collections on CD-ROM or directly from Web sites.
- You can create your own images. For example, you can take digital photos and then use a program such as Adobe Photoshop or Macromedia Fireworks to modify and optimize your images for the Web. You can also create images that aren't based on a photograph. Photoshop and Fireworks are two popular programs that you can use to create your own Web graphics.

File formats

The three main image formats currently supported by browsers are GIF, JPEG, and PNG. *GIF* images can contain a maximum of 256 colors, and they're best suited for images with relatively few colors and areas of flat color, such as line drawings, logos, and illustrations. GIFs also support animation and transparency. The GIF format isn't recommended for photographs or illustrations with complex color gradations. GIF uses a *lossless* compression algorithm, which means that no image data is discarded to compress the image.

The *JPEG* format supports more than 16 million colors, so it's best for photographs and images that have many subtle color shadings. JPEG uses *lossy* compression, which means that some image data is discarded when the file is saved. You can select the degree of compression applied when saving the file, with the following tradeoff: the smaller the file, the lower the image quality.

PNG combines some of the best features of JPEG and GIF. It supports more than 16 million colors, so it's ideal for photos and complex drawings. It can use a variety of lossless compression algorithms and supports many levels of transparency, allowing areas of an image to appear transparent or semi-transparent. The downside of PNG is that some older browsers don't support it.

The following table summarizes these three image file formats.

	GIF	**JPEG**	**PNG**
Best used for	Simple images with few colors	Photographs	Photographs or simple images
Maximum colors	256	More than 16 million	More than 16 million
Compression	Lossless	Lossy	Lossless
Transparency	1 level (complete transparency)	Not supported	Multiple levels
Browser support	All	All	Netscape 6 and later, Internet Explorer 7 and later, Firefox, Safari

Image properties

When you drag an image to a page, SharePoint Designer writes the HTML code required to embed the image. This code, as shown in Exhibit 5-1, consists of the `<img>` (image) tag and several attributes. The location of the `<img>` tag tells the browser where to embed the file, and the `src` attribute tells the browser where to find the image file. The `style` attribute provides the width and height dimensions. This attribute isn't required for the browser to display the image, but providing the image's actual width and height dimensions allows the browser to reserve the proper amount of space for the image and continue to render the rest of the page, which can help the page load faster.

```
<img src="images/logo.gif" style="width: 305px; height: 128px" />
```

Exhibit 5-1: An example of an image tag

After you add an image to a page, you can view and/or update its properties either directly in the HTML code, by using the Picture Properties dialog box or the Tag Properties pane.

Image dimensions

You can change the dimensions of an image by specifying other width and height values, but it's generally not a good idea to do so. If you need to resize an image, you should do so outside of SharePoint Designer in an image editing application, such as Adobe Photoshop or Macromedia Fireworks. Changing the dimensions of an image by modifying its properties in SharePoint Designer has the following drawbacks:

- Unless you change both settings proportionally, the image gets distorted. For example, if an image is 275 pixels wide by 344 pixels high, and you change the width to 290, you must set the height to 362 to retain the proportions.
- If you enlarge the image too much, it appears pixilated. The square pixels that comprise an image become large enough to be seen individually, as demonstrated in Exhibit 5-2.
- If you shrink the image too much, the quality of the image might suffer, and it might become difficult for the user to tell what it is. Reducing the image's dimensions also doesn't decrease its file size, so there's no benefit in terms of download time.

Exhibit 5-2: An enlarged and original version of an image

Do it!

A-1: Exploring image properties

Here's how	Here's why
1 Open the Outlander site	Choose File, Open Site, navigate to the current unit folder, and open the Outlander folder.
Open index.htm	From the Folder List pane.
2 Right-click the "Spice of the Month" image	
Choose **Picture Properties…**	To open the Picture Properties dialog box. The General tab is active by default.
Observe the Picture box	The box shows the file path for the image, which indicates that it's located in the images folder within the root folder for the defined site.
3 Activate the Appearance tab	The Appearance tab shows wrapping and layout attributes, along with the image width and height.
4 Click **Cancel**	To close the dialog box. You can also view image properties by using either the Tag Properties pane or by viewing the HTML code.
5 In the Tag Properties pane, point to <img>	A pop-up message appears, showing the file path, the width, and height for the image.
6 Scroll through the list of available image attributes	(In the Tag Properties pane.) Attributes that are applied by default are highlighted in blue.

Alternate text

Explanation

Alternate text is text you can assign to an image so that viewers with alternative browsers such as screen readers or Braille devices can get an idea of how the image relates in context with the page. It also provides a temporary safeguard in case there's a problem with the image and the browser can't display it. In some browsers, including Internet Explorer, alternate text appears as a screen tip when you point to the image, as shown in Exhibit 5-3. If the browser can't load the image for some reason, the alternate text is still visible within the missing image placeholder.

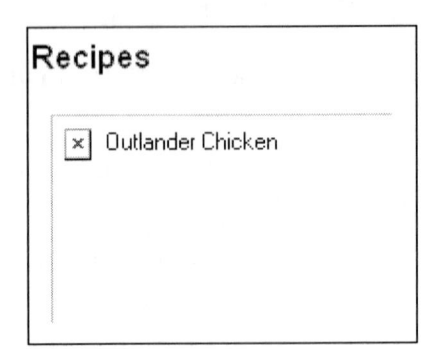

Exhibit 5-3: Alternate text displayed as a screen tip (left) and within a missing image placeholder (right)

You aren't required to specify alternate text for images, but it's a good idea to do so every time you insert an image. It's a small step toward ensuring that your pages are accessible for as many users as possible. When you insert an image, SharePoint Designer automatically opens the Accessibility Properties dialog box, unless you specify that you don't want it to open automatically. To add alternate text to an image that you previously didn't specify alternate text for, first select the image. In the Tag Properties pane, in the alt box, enter the alternate text and press Enter. You can also add alternate text by using the Picture Properties dialog box.

Do it!

A-2: Specifying alternate text

Here's how	Here's why
1 Click the "Spice of the Month" image	(If necessary.) To select it.
2 In the Tag Properties pane, click as shown	![Attributes panel showing src, style, accesskey, align, alt, atomics] Next to the alt attribute.
Type **Spice of the Month** and press ⏎ ENTER	To add alternate text to the image.
3 At the top of the Tag Properties pane, point to <img>	The file path and width and height values are displayed, as well as the alternate text you specified.
4 Save the document and preview the page in Internet Explorer	
5 Point to the "Spice of the Month" image	After a moment, a screen tip appears, showing the alternate text.
6 Close the browser	To return to SharePoint Designer.

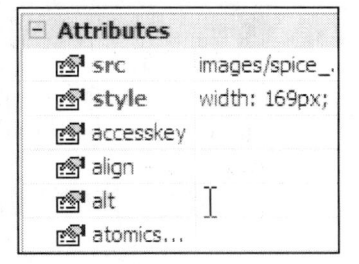

Image-based text

Explanation

If you apply a decorative font face to your text, it's likely that a significant number of users don't have that same font on their computers and would, therefore, be unable to view the text as you intended.

To get around this problem, you can use image-based text. If you have a graphics application, such as Adobe Photoshop or Macromedia Fireworks, you can design text with an exotic font and save it as a GIF image for use as a logo or as headings. With image-based text you can create a wider variety of text styles—styles that can't be achieved by using HTML or CSS, as illustrated in Exhibit 5-4.

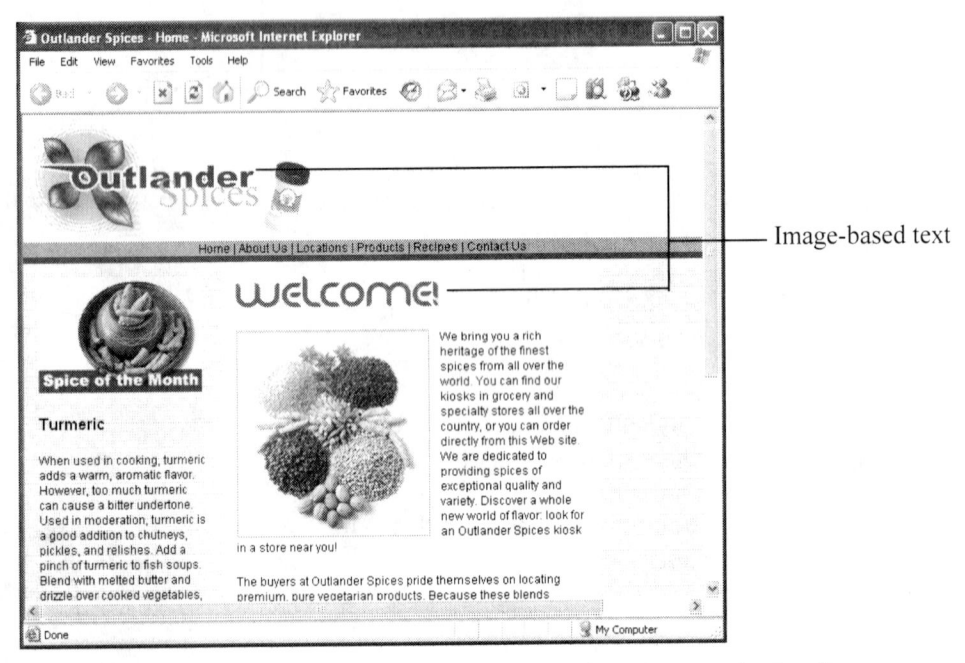

Exhibit 5-4: An example of image-based text used for a logo and a heading

Image-based text does have some disadvantages. Images increase a page's overall size and download time. Using too many of these images can make a page exceedingly slow for some users. Also, because they aren't actual text, the content isn't searchable by search engines or the browser's Find function. However, you can minimize this limitation by specifying alternate text for your images. When specifying alternate text for image-based text, it's a good idea to repeat the text that's in the image so that search engines can locate the content.

Do it!

A-3: Applying image-based text

Here's how	Here's why
1 In the Folder List pane, expand the images folder	
2 From the Folder List pane, drag welcome.gif in front of the word "Welcome," as shown	To insert the image in this location.
In the Alternate text box, type **Welcome**	With image-based text, it's important to specify alternate text that duplicates the text content in the image, so that all users can access the content. Also, search engines can locate alt text, but not text inside an image.
Click **OK**	
3 Delete the text, "Welcome to Outlander Spices"	
4 Save the document, and preview the page in Internet Explorer	Image-based text provides a way to display text in exotic fonts that most users won't likely have on their computers.
5 Close the browser	To return to SharePoint Designer.

Topic B: Working with images

Explanation

After you've added images to a page and applied some basic properties, you probably need to arrange them in relation to other content in your page. The best way to arrange Web page content, including images, is to use CSS styles.

Images and layout

One way to arrange images in a layout is to *float* the image to the left or right of adjacent content by using the float property. For example, Exhibit 5-5 shows an image that's wrapped in a `<div>` tag along with other text content. The image floats to the right of its container, as opposed to the left or right side of the page. The text that's adjacent to the image wraps around the left side of the image. The opposite would be true if the image was floated to the left—adjacent text would wrap around its right side.

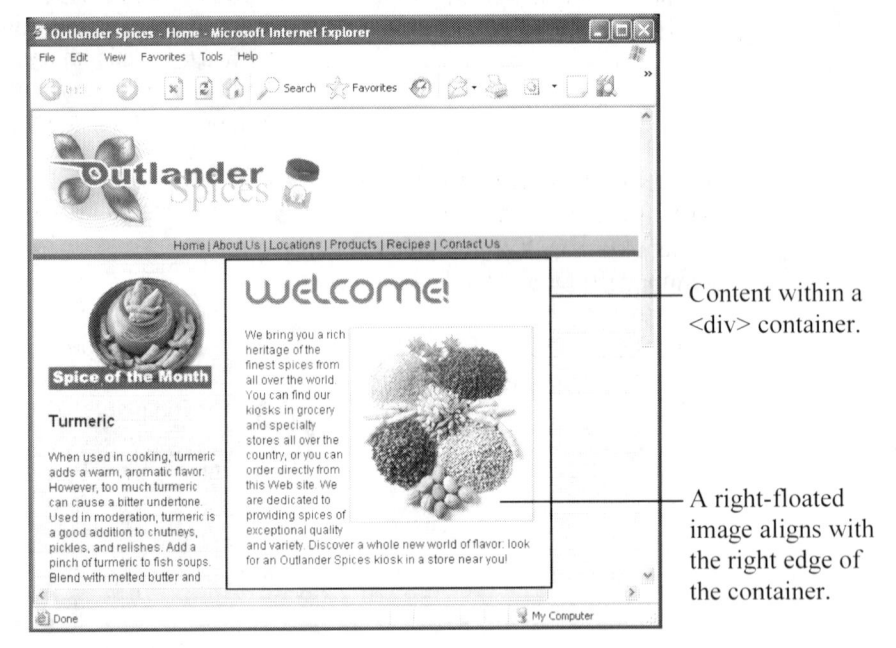

Exhibit 5-5: An example of an image arranged by using CSS

Images   5–11

Do it!

B-1: Arranging images

Here's how	Here's why
1 Click the spices image in the center of the page	To select it. You'll make the text flow around the right side of the image.
2 In the Apply Styles pane, click **New Style**	To open the New Style dialog box.
3 In the Selector box, enter **.imageLeft**	(Be sure to include the period at the beginning of the style name.) You'll use a class style rather than an element style, because an element style would apply to all images, and you want to apply the style only to the spice image.
Define the style in the existing style sheet globalstyles.css	(From the Define in list, select Existing style sheet. Then, click the Browse button and navigate to the location of the globalstyles.css style sheet.) To position the image, you'll float to the left side of its container.
4 Check **Apply new style to document selection**	(At the top of the dialog box.) To apply the style automatically to the selected image.
5 From the Category list, select **Layout**	
From the float list, select **left**	
Click **OK**	To close the dialog box. All the content that was previously in line with the image now wraps around its right side.
6 Drag chicken.jpg before the word "Each," as shown	![chicken image with text "ly Recipes" and "Each sent to us by our customers. T for Outlander Chicken. Check"]
	(Drag the image from the images folder in the Folder List pane.) You'll arrange this image to the right side of its container.
In the Alternate text box, type **Chicken dish**	To describe the content of the image for users with non-visual browsers.
Click **OK**	
7 Click the chicken image	To select it.

8	In the Apply Styles pane, click **New Style**	To open the New Style dialog box.
9	In the Selector box, enter **.imageRight**	
	Verify that globalstyles.css is selected in the URL box	
10	Check **Apply new style to document selection**	To apply the style automatically to the selected image.
11	From the Category list, select **Layout**	
	From the float list, select **right**	
	Click **OK**	To close the dialog box. All the content that was previously in line with the image now wraps around its left side.
12	Save the document	
	Click **OK**	To save the style sheet.
13	Preview the page in Internet Explorer	Press F12.
	Resize the browser window slightly	The text flows around the images when you resize the browser window. Also, notice that the text in the first paragraph directly abuts the spices image. You'll fix this in the next activity.
14	Close the browser	To return to SharePoint Designer.

Image margins

Explanation

When you arrange an image relative to text, it's likely that some of the text abuts the edge of the image, making it difficult to read, as shown in Exhibit 5-6. To add some space between an image and the text that wraps around it, you can apply a margin to one or more sides of the image.

Exhibit 5-6: An example of adding a margin to the right side of an image

Do it!

B-2: Adding margins to images

Here's how	Here's why
1 In the Apply Styles pane, right-click **.imageLeft**	Scroll down, if necessary.
Choose **Modify Style...**	To open the Modify Style dialog box. You'll add a margin style to the image to create some space between the images and the text that wraps around them.
2 From the Category list, select **Box**	The box properties of CSS include margin and padding attributes.
3 To the right of margin, clear **Same for all**	So that you can apply margin styles to individual sides of the image, rather than the same values on all four sides.
4 In the right box, enter **10**	To apply a 10-pixel margin on the right side of the image.
5 Click **OK**	Some space appears between the spice image and the text, making it more readable and generally more professional looking.
6 In the Apply Styles pane, right-click **.imageRight**	
Choose **Modify Style...**	To open the Modify Style dialog box.
From the Category list, select **Box**	
To the right of margin, clear **Same for all**	
In the left box, enter **10** and click **OK**	The text re-wraps around the image to accommodate the new margin.
7 Save the document	
Click **OK**	To save the style sheet.

Borders and padding

Explanation

Occasionally, you might want to add a border to an image for design reasons or perhaps to emphasize it or visually separate it from adjacent content. You can apply a variety of border styles and colors to your page elements, including images.

Exhibit 5-7: An example of a border around an image

You can also apply padding to your page elements. *Padding* increases the space between an element's content and its borders. An element doesn't need to have visible borders to make padding effective, however. If an element has no border, and you apply padding to the image, you increase the space between the element and adjacent elements. The difference between padding and margins is that margins apply space around an element starting from outside the element's border.

Do it!

B-3: Adding image borders and padding

Here's how	Here's why
1 In the Apply Styles pane, right-click **.imageLeft**	
Choose **Modify Style...**	You'll apply a border to the image.
2 From the Category list, select **Border**	
Below border-style, from the top list, select **ridge**	The Preview window displays an example of the selected border style.
Below border-width, from the top list, select **thin**	The Preview window updates to reflect a thin ridge border.
Below border-color, from the top list, select a green color	
3 From the Category list, select **Box**	
Next to padding, verify that Same for all is checked	You'll apply padding to all four sides of the image.
In the top box, enter **5**	
4 Click **OK**	To close the dialog box and apply the style. The image now has 5 pixels of padding on all four sides.
5 Save the document	
Click **OK**	To update the style sheet.
Preview the page in Internet Explorer	
6 Close the browser window	To return to SharePoint Designer.
7 Save and close any open files	
Choose **File**, **Close Site**	To close the Outlander Web site.

Unit summary: Images

Topic A In this topic, you learned the differences between **image formats**, and you learned how to adjust basic **image properties**. You also learned how to apply **alternate text** to an image. You learned that it's important to use alternate text to ensure that users with non-visual browsers understand the context of the image relative to the page content.

Topic B In this topic, you learned how to use the **float** property to **arrange images** relative to adjacent content, and you learned how to apply **margins**, **borders**, and **padding** to an element.

Independent practice activity

In this activity, you'll apply alternate text to images and use CSS styles to arrange images within a container. You'll also modify an existing style by adding a border to an image.

1. From the Practice folder in the current unit folder, open **index.htm**.
2. Apply appropriate alternate text to the three images on the page.
3. Replace the text, "Welcome to Outlander Spices," with the welcome.gif image. (The image is located in the images subfolder.)
4. Create a class style that floats an element to the left of its container. (You'll apply this style to the spices image.) Include a right margin to create some room between the image and the adjacent content.
5. Apply the class style to the spices image (the first image in the right column). The image should look similar to the example shown in Exhibit 5-8.
6. Create another class style that floats an element to the right of its container. (You'll apply the style to the chicken image.) Include a left margin to create some room between the image and the adjacent content.
7. Apply the style to the chicken image. The image should look similar to the example shown in Exhibit 5-9.
8. Apply a border style, width, and color of your choice to the spice image under the Welcome heading.
9. Save and close all open files.
10. Close the site.

Exhibit 5-8: The home page after step 5

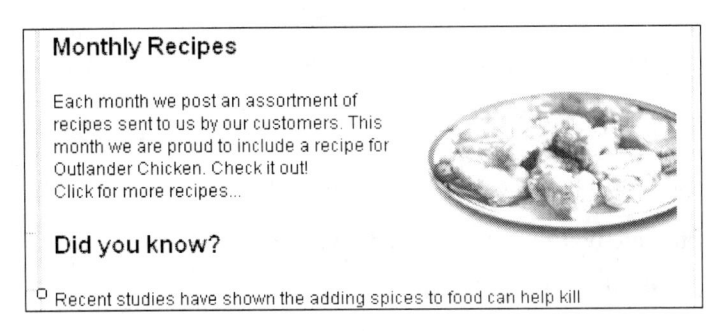

Exhibit 5-9: The home page after step 7

Review questions

1 Which of the following are advantages of using image-based text?

   A Image-based text allows you to use uncommon fonts and text effects.

   B Image-based text loads faster than normal text.

   C Image-based text is more accessible than actual text.

   D Image-based text is easier to read than normal text.

2 What's a potential drawback to using image-based text instead of actual text?

3 Alternate text for a photograph should:

   A describe the content of the image.

   B duplicate any text that appears in the image.

   C be omitted.

   D indicate that it's a photographic image.

4 Alternate text for image-based text should:

   A describe the content of the image.

   B duplicate the text in the image.

   C be omitted.

   D indicate that it's image-based text.

5 True or false? When you float an element to one side, any adjacent content wraps to the opposite side.

6 True or false? Margins create space between an element and its borders.

Unit 6
Hyperlinks

Unit time: 45 minutes

Complete this unit, and you'll know how to:

A Create links, link bars, e-mail links, and bookmark links.

B Customize link styles.

C Create an image map.

Topic A: Basic hyperlinks

Explanation

Hyperlinks provide the essential functionality that makes the Web the interconnected world that it is. These hyperlinks, or just links, allow users to navigate a Web site, open external pages and resources such as multimedia files, and jump to specific sections of a page.

Link types

There are three basic link types:

- **Local** links navigate to pages and resources in the same Web site.
- **External** links navigate to pages and resources outside of the Web site.
- **Bookmark** links navigate to specific sections of a page. Bookmarks are also referred to as *anchors* or *intra-document links*.

By default, most browsers display links as blue, underlined text, but you can change this default style.

Local links

Local links are links to pages and resources within your Web site, so specifying the path is relatively simple. To create a local link:

1. Select the text or image that you want to use for the link.
2. In the Standard toolbar, click the Insert Hyperlink button. The Insert Hyperlink dialog box appears, as shown in Exhibit 6-1. By default, the contents of the site folder are visible.
3. In the Text to display box, verify that the link text is accurate. If you're using text for the hyperlink, the selected text appears in the box. If you're using an image for the hyperlink, the box is inactive.
4. From the list, select the destination page for the link. (You might need to navigate to a subfolder to select the page.) When you select the destination page, the file path for the page appears in the Address box.
5. Click OK to create the link.

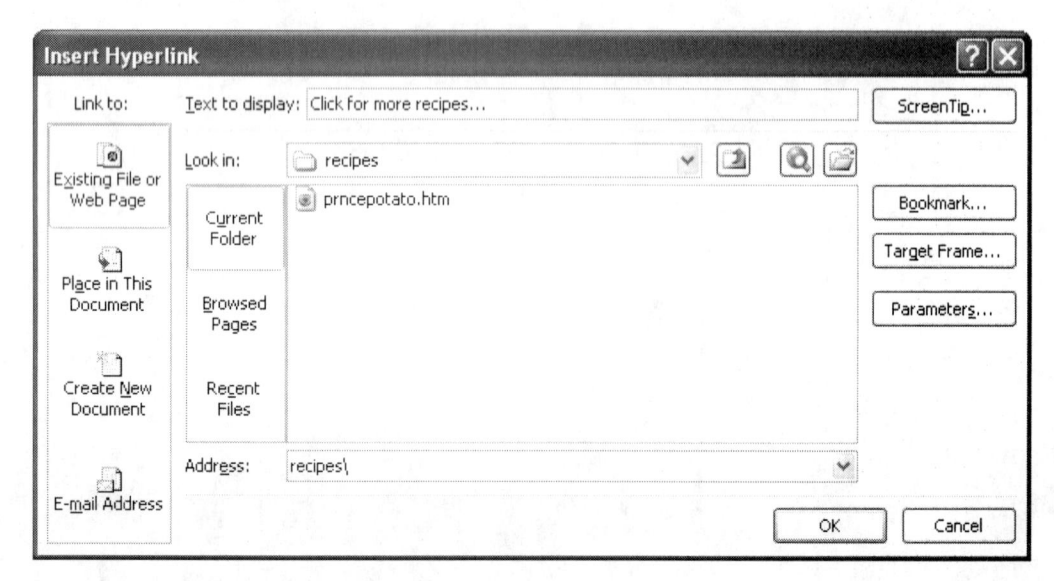

Exhibit 6-1: The Insert Hyperlink dialog box

Do it!

A-1: Creating a local link

Here's how	Here's why
1 Open the Outlander site	From the current unit folder.
2 Open index.htm	
3 Select the text **Click for more recipes...**	us by our customers. This r include a recipe for Outland [p] Click for more recipes... **Did you know?**
4 In the Common toolbar, click	(The Insert Hyperlink button). To open the Insert Hyperlink dialog box. The center pane shows the contents of the root folder.
In the list, click **recipes.htm**	To specify the link target.
Click **OK**	
5 Observe the text	[p] Click for more recipes... In most browsers, links appear as blue, underlined text by default to distinguish them from normal text.
6 Save the page and preview it in Internet Explorer	
7 Test the link	(Click it.) The browser opens the recipes page.
8 Close the browser	

Link bars

Explanation

A well-designed Web site should provide a set of navigational links so that users can easily access the information they're looking for. Most sites do this by placing a consistent navigation bar at the top of each page, similar to the example shown in Exhibit 6-2. For large sites with many pages, the navigation bar might be divided into categories based on the different types of information contained in the site. Clicking a top-level link in the navigation bar might expand a submenu of additional links.

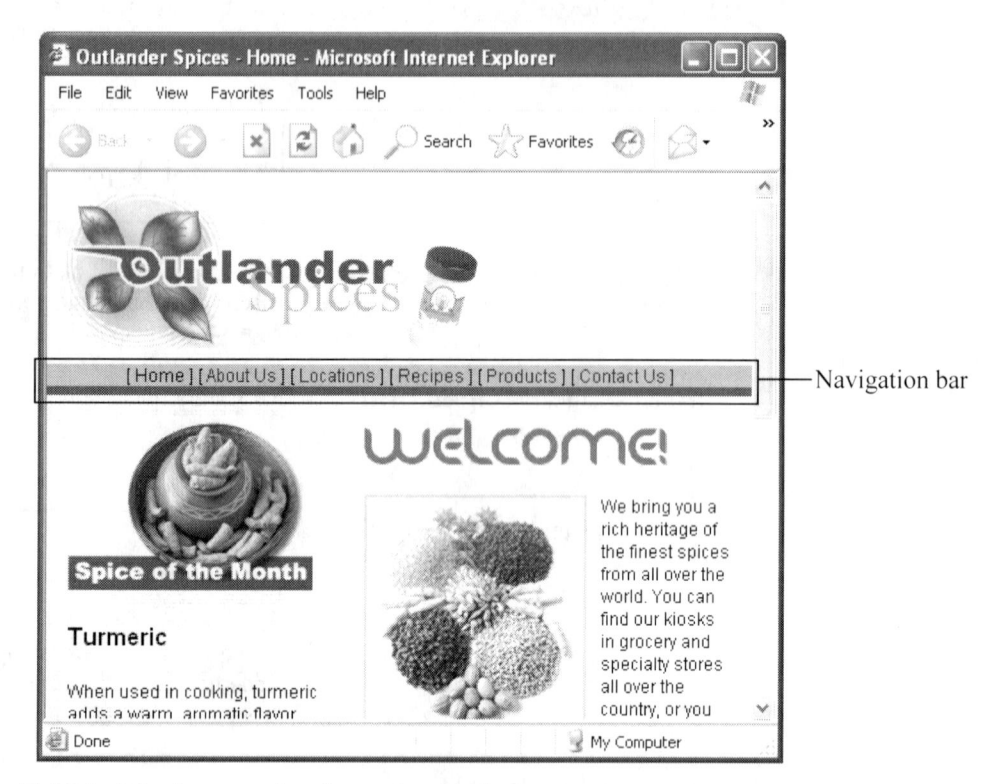

Exhibit 6-2: An example of a navigation bar

Creating a navigation or link bar can be time consuming, especially if you need to duplicate the links on each page. SharePoint Designer makes the process more efficient by including a Link Bar component you can use to generate and maintain a navigation bar automatically. You can use this component to generate the links you need, apply styles to the links, and establish the navigation bar's layout on the page.

To create a link bar:

1 Choose Insert, Web Component. The Insert Web Component dialog box appears.
2 Under Component Type, select Link Bars. All link bar components are visible in the right pane.
3 Select Bar with custom links, and click Next.
4 Select a bar style from the list or choose to use the page's current theme (the top default selection). Click Next.
5 Choose an orientation for the navigation bar (either horizontal or vertical) and click Finish. If this is the first navigation bar you've created since installing SharePoint Designer, the Create New Link bar dialog box appears.
6 Enter a descriptive name for the link bar and click OK to view the Link Bar Properties dialog box, as shown in Exhibit 6-3.

7 To create a link to the Home page, under Additional links, check Home page.
8 Click Add Link. The Add to Link Bar dialog box appears.
9 Enter the text for the link and the page you want to link to and click OK.
10 Repeat the process for the other links you want to include in the link bar.
11 Click OK.

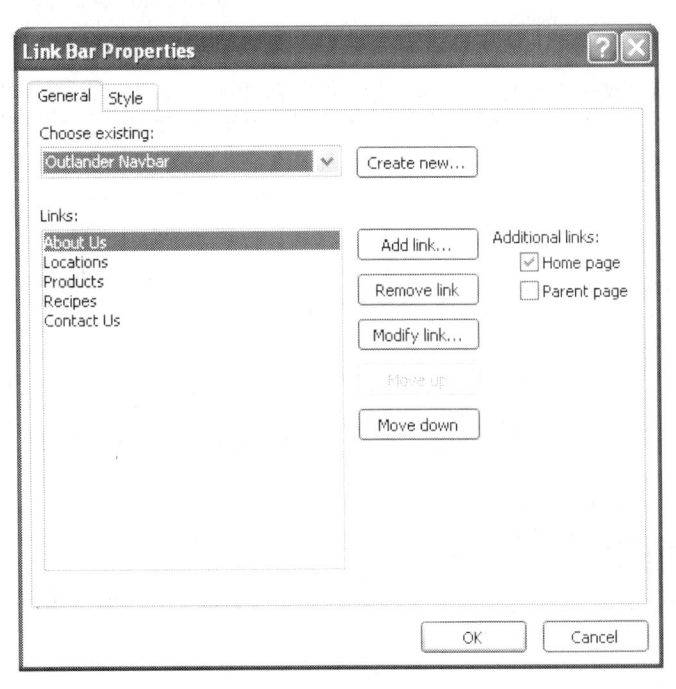

Exhibit 6-3: The Link Bar Properties dialog box

Do it!

A-2: Creating a link bar

Here's how	Here's why
1 Open the Outlander template	(From the templates subfolder.) You'll create a navigation bar for every page in the site.
Triple-click the text in the navigation bar	To select it.
Press ← BACKSPACE	To delete the text. You'll create a new link bar by using a Web component.
2 Choose **Insert, Web Component...**	To open the Insert Web Component dialog box.
3 Under Component type, click **Link Bars**	Three link bar options are visible in the right pane. You'll manually define the links for the link bar.

4	Under Choose a bar type, click **Bar with custom links**	If necessary.
5	Click **Next**	The dialog box changes to show a list of themes you can use for the links. You can either create text links or use preset images. You want to use styles already defined within the site, so you'll leave the default selection.
6	Click **Next**	The dialog box shows two link bar orientation types: horizontal or vertical. You'll create a horizontal link bar.
7	Click **Finish**	The Create New Link Bar dialog box appears.
8	Type **mainLinks**	To name the navigation bar.
	Click **OK**	The Link Bar Properties dialog box appears. Next, you'll define the links in the link bar.
9	Under Additional links, check **Home page**	To specify a link to the home page (index.htm).
10	Click **Add link...**	To open the Add to Link Bar dialog box, which is similar to the Insert Hyperlink dialog box you worked with earlier.
	In the Text to display box, enter **About Us**	This is the text that will appear in the link bar.
	In the file list, click **aboutus.htm** and click **OK**	To create the first link.
11	Create a second link named Locations	Use locations.htm as the target for the link.
12	Click **OK**	To close the dialog box. The link bar appears in the green container. Each link is blue and underlined by default. Also, brackets are automatically added around each link. You can change these styles as needed.
13	Save the template	
	Click **Yes**, and then click **Close**	To update the attached files.
14	Switch to index.htm	The link bar appears in the same location. Because this is the home page (index.htm), the Home link isn't active.
15	Save the document	If necessary.

External links and e-mail links

Explanation

External links navigate to a page or resource on another Web site. You can also create a link that opens the user's default e-mail program and starts an outgoing message. Then you can append the e-mail address of your choice in the To: field.

To create an external link:

1 Select the text (or image) that you want to use for the link.
2 In the Standard toolbar, click the Insert Hyperlink button to open the Insert Hyperlinks dialog box.
3 In the Text to display box, verify that the link text is accurate.
4 In the Address box, enter the URL of the Web page.
5 Click OK.

If you've recently viewed the page you want to link to, you can also click Browsed Pages to view a history of recently visited pages, and then click the URL of the page you want to link to.

To create an e-mail link:

1 Select the text (or image) that you want to use for the link.
2 In the Standard toolbar, click the Insert Hyperlink button to open the Insert Hyperlinks dialog box.
3 In the Text to display box, verify that the link text is accurate.
4 Under Link to, select E-mail Address. The dialog box changes to show options for e-mail links, as shown in Exhibit 6-4.
5 Enter the e-mail address in the E-mail address box. When you begin typing, the prefix "mailto:" is automatically appended in front of the address. This triggers the browser to open the user's default email program when the link is clicked.
6 If you want to add a default subject line to the e-mail message, enter it in the Subject box.
7 Click OK.

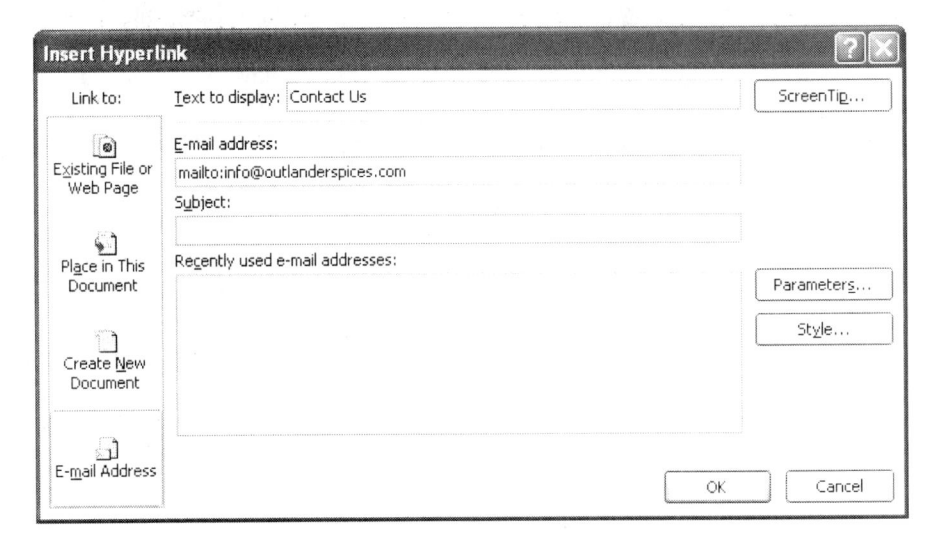

Exhibit 6-4: Creating an e-mail link

If no e-mail application is configured on the user's computer when an e-mail link is clicked, a dialog box appears, prompting the user to configure an e-mail application.

Update a link bar

After you've created a link bar, you might want to modify it or add new links to it. To modify a link bar, double-click one of the hyperlinks in the link bar to open the Link Bar Properties dialog box. You can then make the desired changes.

Do it!

A-3: Creating external links

Here's how	Here's why
1 Switch to outlander.dwt	You'll create a link that will allow users to contact Outlander Spices via e-mail.
2 Point to a link in the link bar	[Home] [About] [Loca
	The pointer changes to a hand holding a piece of paper. If you want to test a link from within SharePoint Designer, you have to press Ctrl and click.
Double-click one of the links	To open the Link Bar Properties dialog box.
3 Click **Add link…**	You'll add a new link to the link bar.
In the Text to display box, enter **Contact Us**	
4 Under Link to, click **E-mail Address**	(On the left side of the dialog box.) The dialog box changes to show options for e-mail links.
In the E-mail address box, enter **info@outlanderspices.com**	When you begin typing the address, the prefix "mailto:" is appended automatically.
Click **OK**	The Contact Us link appears below the About Us link in the list. You'll make the Contact Us link the last link in the link bar.
5 Click **Contact Us**	(If necessary.) To select it.
Click **Move Down**	Links: About Us Locations Contact Us
	To move the entry to the bottom of the list.
6 Click **OK**	To close the dialog box. When a user clicks the link, his or her default e-mail program opens with this address appended to the outgoing message.
7 Save the template	
Click **Yes** and then click **Close**	To update the attached files.
8 Open aboutus.htm	You'll link an image to an external Web site.

9	Scroll down and select the indicated image	
		You'll link this image to the iso.org Web site.
10	In the Common toolbar, click	To open the Insert Hyperlink dialog box.
11	Under Link to, click **Existing File or Web Page**	
	In the Address box, enter **http://www.iso.org**	
	Click **OK**	To create the link.
12	Switch to Split view	To view the code for the linked image. By default, SharePoint Designer inserts a style rule in the `<img>` tag, which disables the default blue border with which linked images normally appear.
	Switch to Design view	
13	Save the document and preview it in Internet Explorer	
14	In the navigation bar, click **Home**	To open the Home page.
	In the navigation bar, click **About Us**	To return to the About Us page.
15	Click the ISO 9000 image	(Scroll down, if necessary.) The browser is directed to the ISO Web site.
	Click the Back button	To return to the About Us page.
16	In the navigation bar, click **Contact Us**	An e-mail message with the specified address opens in the default e-mail application. (If no e-mail application is configured, you're prompted to configure an e-mail application.)
	Close the e-mail message	If applicable.
17	Close the browser	To return to SharePoint Designer.

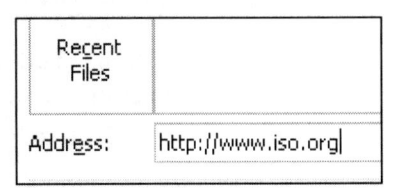

Bookmarks

Explanation

You can use a *bookmark* to create a link to a specific section of a Web page. To do this, you insert a bookmark in a page and then create a link to the bookmark. Bookmarks are particularly useful for long pages with a lot of text.

To create a bookmark:

1. Select the text (or image) that you want to use for the bookmark.
2. Choose Insert, Bookmark. The Bookmark dialog box appears. By default, the text you selected is used for the bookmark name. Any spaces between words in the text are replaced with underscores. You can use a different name for the bookmark name, but it's generally easier to manage if you use the same text.
3. Click OK. Bookmarked text appears with a thin dotted line beneath it.

To create a link to a bookmark:

1. Select the text (or image) that you want to use for the link.
2. In the Standard toolbar, click the Insert Hyperlink button to open the Insert Hyperlinks dialog box.
3. In the Text to display box, verify that the link text is accurate.
4. Under Link to, click Place in This Document. The dialog box changes to show a complete list of bookmarks included in the page, as shown in Exhibit 6-5.
5. From the list of bookmarks, select the bookmark to which you want to link and click OK to create the link.

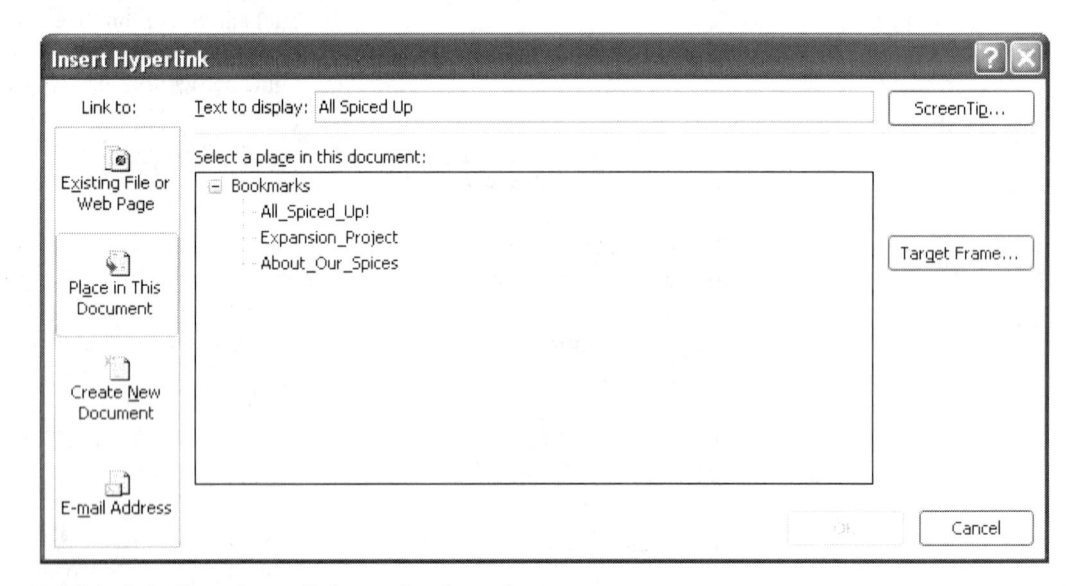

Exhibit 6-5: Creating a link to a bookmark

Hyperlinks **6–11**

Do it! **A-4: Creating and linking to bookmarks**

Here's how	Here's why
1 Select the large green heading **All Spiced Up!**	(At the top of the About Us page.) You'll create bookmark links within the page, so that users can navigate to a specific section of the page by clicking one of the subject headings at the top. First, you'll create the necessary bookmarks.
2 Choose **Insert**, **Bookmark...**	[Bookmark dialog showing Bookmark name: All_Spiced_Up!] To open the Bookmark dialog box. By default, the bookmark name appears as All_Spiced_Up!
Click **OK**	[Image showing All Spiced Up! heading with h1 tag] To create the bookmark. The text appears with a dashed underline to indicate that it's a bookmark. This style appears only while working in SharePoint Designer—it isn't present when viewed in a browser.
3 Switch to Split view, and observe the code for the selected text	The text is enclosed in <a> tags (anchor tags). The name attribute defines the name of the bookmark. This is commonly referred to as a "named anchor." It doesn't appear or function as a normal link, but it acts as a target for internal links.
4 Switch to Design view	

5	Select the heading **Expansion Project**	Scroll down to locate the heading, and triple-click the text.
	Press CTRL + G	To open the Bookmark dialog box. Expansion_Project appears by default in the Bookmark name box.
	Click **OK**	To create the bookmark.
6	Create a new bookmark for the heading **About Our Spices**	(Scroll down.) Next, you'll create links to the bookmarks you've created.
7	Scroll to the top of the page	
	Select the text **All Spiced Up**, as shown	Be sure not to select the text that defines the bookmark.
8	In the Standard toolbar, click [icon]	(Or press Ctrl+K.) To open the Insert Hyperlink dialog box.
9	Under Link to, click **Place in This Document**	The center pane shows the existing bookmarks in the page.
	From the list of bookmarks, select **All_Spiced_Up!**	To link to this bookmark.
	Click **OK**	To create the link. The selected text appears blue and underlined, indicating that it's a link. You'll learn how to customize link styles later in this unit.

10	In the Tag Properties pane, point to the <a> tag	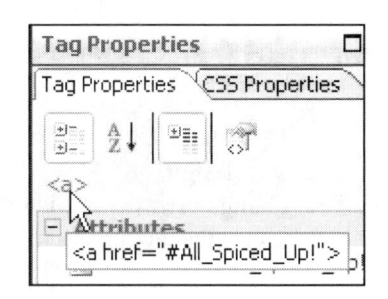 The `href` attribute shows the link target. Bookmark references must begin with the number sign (#).
11	Select the text **Expansion Project**	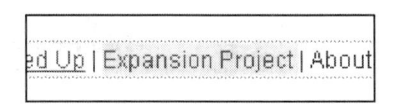 At the top of the page.
	Link the text to the bookmark within the page	Press Ctrl+K. From the Bookmarks list, select Expansion_Project, and click OK.
12	Select the text **About Our Spices**	
	Link it to its bookmark	
13	Save the page and preview it in Internet Explorer	Notice that all links appear as purple, underlined text. This is the default color for visited links. Because the bookmark link targets are all part of this current page, they appear as visited.
14	Click **All Spiced Up!**	The target heading (the "bookmark") appears at the top of the browser window.
	Scroll to the top of the page and test the other two bookmarks	You could also copy and paste the links at the bottom of the page, allowing users to navigate to specific text from either the top or bottom of the page.
15	Close the browser	To return to SharePoint Designer.

Topic B: Link styles

Explanation

By default, links appear as blue, underlined text. These default styles might suit your site design, but if they aren't complementary to your site's color scheme, you can change their color and other aspects of their appearance. You can use CSS to assign styles that act as visual cues to the state of a link.

Link states

Link states define the current condition of a link. There are four link states, as described in the following table.

State	Description
link	The default state of a link that hasn't been activated in any way.
hover	A link enters the hover state when you point to it. Most browsers don't apply any default formatting to the hover state.
active	The state of a link when you click the link but haven't yet released the mouse button. A link is in this state only for a moment. Most browsers don't apply any default formatting to the active state.
visited	The state of a link after you click it, and its destination page has loaded. In most browsers, visited links appear as purple, underlined text by default.

Visited links

The browser's cache keeps track of links whose destinations have already been viewed. When a link has been visited, the link remains in that state unless the browser's cache is cleared. In Internet Explorer, you can choose Tools, Internet Options, Clear History to reset the browser's list of visited links.

If you recently viewed the page that a link references, it appears in the visited state, even if you didn't click the link.

Hyperlinks **6–15**

Do it! **B-1: Formatting links**

Here's how	Here's why
1 Observe the links in the navigation bar	SharePoint Designer displays links as blue, underlined text, consistent with the default styles that most browsers use. You'll customize the default appearance of text links and apply styles to the hover and visited states.
2 In the Apply Styles pane, click **New Style**	To open the New Style dialog box.
3 From the Selector list, select **a:link**	To define the default appearance of links that haven't yet been clicked.
Define the style in the external style sheet globalstyles.css	From the Define in list, select Existing style sheet, and browser to the globalstyles.css style sheet, in the styles folder.
4 In the Font category, under text-decoration, check **none**	text-decoration: ☐ underline ☐ overline ☐ line-through ☐ blink ☑ none To disable the default underlining for this link state.
In the Font category, from the color list, select **More Colors...**	
Select a dark green color	
From the font-weight list, select **bold**	
Click **OK**	By default, the links now appear as bold, dark green text.

5 In the Apply Styles pane, click **New Style**

From the Selector list, select **a:hover**

Verify that the style will be created in globalstyles.css

6 In the Font category, under text-decoration, check **underline** | When a user points to a link, it will appear underlined.

In the Font category, from the color list, select **More Colors…**

Select a dark brown color

From the font-weight list, select **bold**

Click **OK** | To see the changes, you need to save your changes and preview the page in Internet Explorer.

7 Create a new style for the visited state | In the Apply Styles pane, click New Style. From the Selector list, select a:visited.

8 In the Font category, from the color list, select **More Colors…**

Select a dark gray color

From the font-weight list, select **bold**

Under text-decoration, check **none**

Click **OK**

9 Save the page and preview it in Internet Explorer | (When you save the page, you're prompted to update the style sheet as well.) Some (or all) links appear gray because you've already visited the pages they reference. To view the links in their original state, you need to clear the browser history.

10	Choose **Tools, Delete Browsing History…**	To open the Delete Browsing History dialog box.
	Click **Delete History**	
	Click **Yes**	To close the alert box.
	Click **Close**	
11	Refresh the page	Now the links appear with the styles you applied to the link states.
12	Point to **Home**	The text changes to brown and underlined, the styles you defined for the hover state.
13	Click **Home**	To open the home page.
	Click **About Us**	To return to the About Us page.
14	Click a blank area of the page	(To deselect the link.) The text appears gray to indicate that the link has been visited.
15	Close the browser	To return to SharePoint Designer.

Topic C: Image maps

Explanation

You can create an image that contains multiple links. You define *hotspots*, which are clickable regions of an image, to create an *image map*. This technique provides a variety of design options and practical applications.

Hotspots

You can create hotspots of many sizes and shapes. For example, in Exhibit 6-6, if you want to make each state a hotspot, you'd need to create a wide variety of hotspot shapes. Each hotspot can link to its own destination.

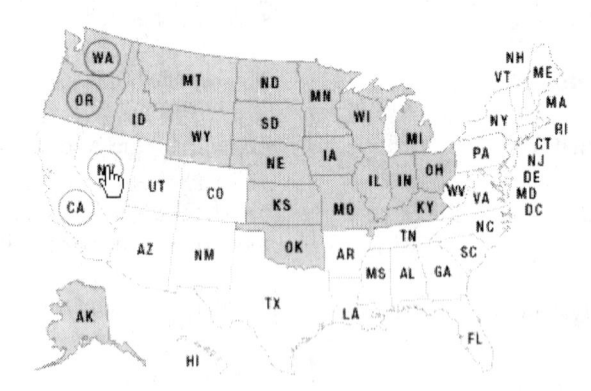

Exhibit 6-6: An image that might be well suited as an image map

To create an image map:

1. Select the image you want to use as the image map.
2. Choose View, Toolbars, Pictures to open the Pictures floating toolbar. You can also right-click an open toolbar and select Pictures.
3. Select one of the hotspot tools: the Rectangular Hotspot tool, the Circular Hotspot tool, or the Polygonal Hotspot tool.
4. Draw the shape to define a hotspot on the image. If you're using the Rectangular or Circular Hotspot tools, you can drag to create the shape. If you're using the Polygonal Hotspot tool, you can click where you want each corner of the shape to be. When you complete the shape, the Insert Hyperlink dialog box appears.
5. Create the hyperlink and click OK.

Do it!

C-1: Creating an image map

Here's how	Here's why
1 Open locations.htm	The page contains an image of the United States, and includes content indicating where patrons can purchase Outlander Spices products. You'll make it an image map that enables users to access store location information.

2	Choose **View**, **Toolbars**, **Pictures**	To open the Pictures toolbar.
	Reposition the toolbar so that the US image is visible	If necessary.
3	Click the US image	To select it. You'll begin by defining a hotspot for the state of Oregon.
4	In the toolbar, click □	The Rectangular Hotspot tool.
5	Point to the top-left corner of the state of Oregon, as shown	
		(The pointer changes to a pencil icon.) You'll create a hotspot so that when a user clicks Oregon, the browser jumps to a corresponding bookmark on the page.
	Begin dragging to the right and down	
		The rectangle defines the clickable region for the link.
	When the rectangle covers most of the state, release the mouse button	The Insert Hyperlink dialog box appears.
6	Under Link to, click **Place in This Document**	(If necessary.) The center pane changes to show any existing bookmarks in the page.
	From the list of bookmarks, select **Oregon**	To link to this bookmark.
	Click **OK**	To create the hyperlink.
7	Is the Rectangular Hotspot tool the best tool for this hotspot? Why or why not?	
8	In the Picture toolbar, click	(The Polygonal Hotspot tool.) You'll create a polygon hotspot.

9	Point to the top-right corner of the state of Nevada, as shown	
		The pointer changes to a pencil icon.
	Click the top-right corner of the state border	To set the first point of the hotspot polygon.
	Click the top-left corner of the state border	
		To define the second point of the polygon. A line appears between the two points.
	Click each corner until the hotspot takes the shape of the state, as shown	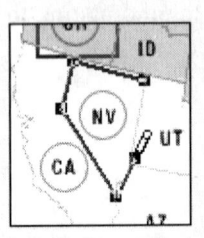
10	Click the starting point	To close the hotspot. The Insert Hyperlink dialog box appears.
11	Select Nevada and click **OK**	
12	Save the page and preview it in Internet Explorer	
13	Point to **OR**	The pointer changes to a pointing finger, indicating that this region is a link.
	Click **OR**	To jump to the list of stores located in Oregon.
	Scroll to the top of the page and test the NV hotspot	
14	Close the browser	To return to SharePoint Designer.
15	Close the Pictures toolbar	
16	Save and close all open documents	
	Choose **File**, **Close Site**	To close the Outlander Web site.

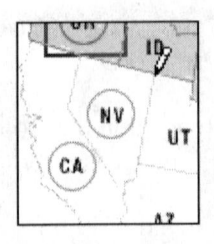

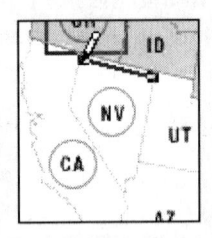

Unit summary: Hyperlinks

Topic A In this topic, you learned about the three basic link types: **internal links**, **external links**, and **bookmark links**. You learned how to create links and create and modify a **link bar** to establish the site's primary navigation. Finally, you learned how to create **external links**, **e-mail links**, and bookmark links.

Topic B In this topic, you learned about the four **link states**; link, hover, active, and visited. You learned how to apply styles to each link state so that the styles complement a design and provide feedback to the user.

Topic C In this topic, you learned how to create an **image map** by defining **hotspots** on an image. You learned how to draw rectangular hotspots and polygonal hotspots, and you linked the hotspots to bookmarks.

Independent practice activity

In this activity, you'll create and link bookmarks to make a page containing a lot of text easier to navigate. You'll also create a link bar for a site, and you'll apply styles to the link, hover, and visited link states. Finally, you'll create an image map.

1. Open the Practice site (from in the current unit folder).
2. Open **aboutus.htm**.
3. Create bookmarks for each level-one (H1) heading in the text.
4. Link the bookmark link text at the top of the page to its corresponding bookmarks.
5. Preview the page in Internet Explorer. Click the links to verify that they work correctly. When you're done, close the browser, and save and close aboutus.htm.
6. Open **outlander.dwt** (from the templates subfolder).
7. Select and delete the navigational text in the navbar container. Insert a new link bar. You want to create links for Home page, About Us, and Locations, and an email link for Contact Us. Use **info@outlanderspices.com** for the email link.
8. Save and close the template and update all pages linked to it.
9. Open **outlanderstyles.css** (in the styles subfolder).
10. Create new element styles to format the link, hover, and visited states for text links. Save the style sheet, when you're finished.
11. Open **locations.htm**.
12. Create hotspots on the image of the United States for each state with a circle on it. As you create each hotspot, link it to the corresponding state text below the image (the bookmarks already exist). (*Hint:* You'll need to open the Picture toolbar to view the hotspot tools.)
13. Save and preview the page in Internet Explorer. Also, preview the links on other pages to make sure they work correctly. If necessary, clear the browser history so that you can view the links in the link bar in the default and hover states.
14. Close the browser to return to SharePoint Designer.
15. Close all open documents. Close the Pictures toolbar if necessary.
16. Close the site.

Review questions

1 Which of the following are types of hyperlinks? (Choose all that apply.)

   A Bookmarks

   B Local

   C Interpage

   D External

   E E-mail

   F Styled

   G Basic

2 How can you create a link bar?

   A Type the text you want for the links, select each portion of text, and create the links you want.

   B Type the text you want for the links, select all the text links, and click the Insert Hyperlink button to open the Link Bar dialog box.

   C Choose Insert, Bookmark and establish the link you want. Repeat the process for each of the links in the link bar.

   D Choose Insert, Web Component, select Link Bars from the category list, and establish the links you want.

3 The hover state is the:

   A default state of a link.

   B state a link enters when you click it.

   C state a link enters when you point to it.

   D state a link enters when it has already been clicked.

4 True or false? When you close a browser after clicking links on a page and then open the same page in a new browser session, the visited links doesn't appear with the visited styles you applied.

5 Which of the following are hotspot tools? (Choose all that apply.)

   A Rectangular Hotspot tool

   B Circular Hotspot tool

   C Triangular Hotspot tool

   D Polygonal Hotspot tool

Unit 7
Tables

Unit time: 45 minutes

Complete this unit, and you'll know how to:

A Insert a table in a page; format table cells, rows, and columns; and create a caption.

B Work with nested tables.

Topic A: Working with tables

Explanation

Presenting data in a table format can be an effective way to organize and display information. For example, a list of products and their prices is often best displayed in a table, because a table structures the data in a familiar and intuitive format, as demonstrated in Exhibit 7-1.

Creating tables

Tables consist of rows and columns with data contained in individual cells. A *cell* is an intersection of a row and a column. If you have ever used a spreadsheet, the cells in a table are similar.

Product Name	Net Weight	Price
Green Cardamom	4 oz.	$3.99
Orange Chilis	6 oz.	$4.49

Exhibit 7-1: A simple table

Exhibit 7-2 shows the individual components of a table, as well as how you might use a table to arrange content on a page.

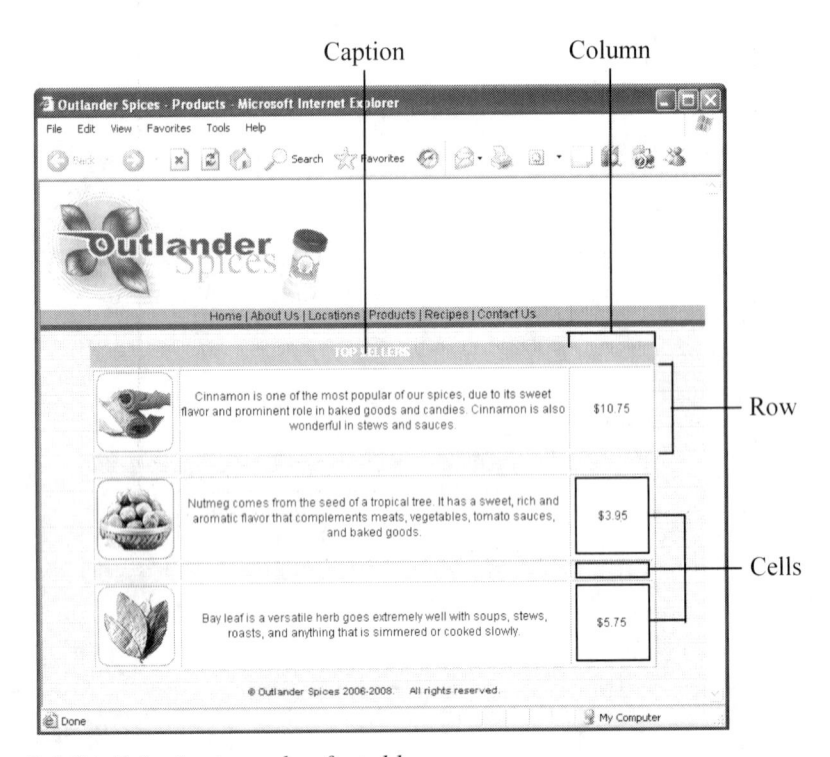

Exhibit 7-2: An example of a table

Inserting a table

You can add a table by using the Insert Table command in the Table menu or by using the table tools to draw a table. To insert a table using the Insert Table command:

1. Place the insertion point where you want to insert the table.
2. Choose Table, Insert Table. The Insert Table dialog box appears, as shown in Exhibit 7-3.
3. In the Rows and Columns boxes, specify the number of rows and columns.
4. Set any other options you want for the table. For example, you can select options under Layout to specify a specific table width or to set the amount of padding or spacing you want between table cells. You can also specify border options and specify a background color or image for the table.
5. Click OK.

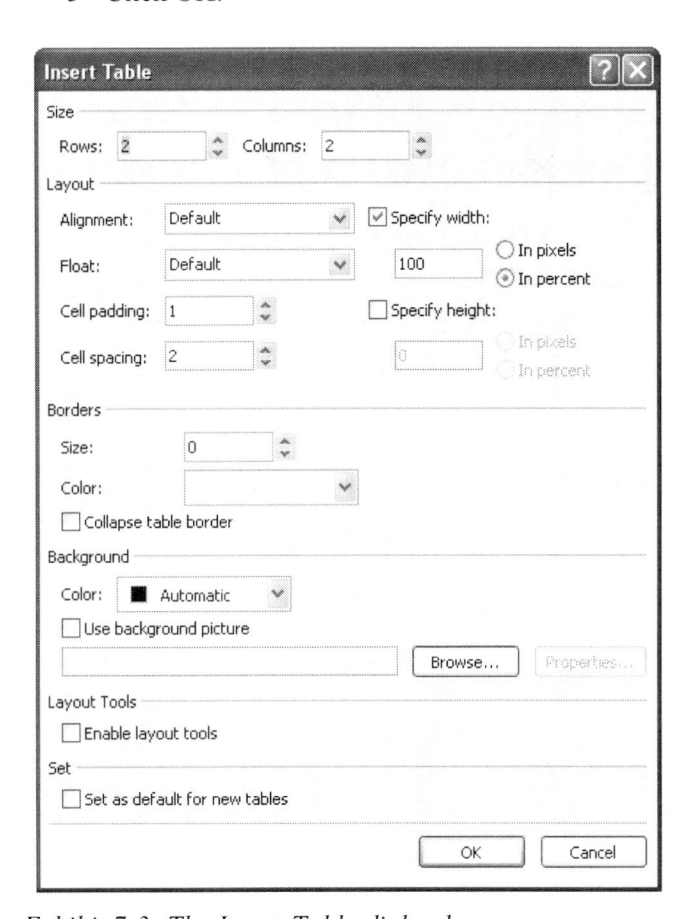

Exhibit 7-3: The Insert Table dialog box

Table tools

You can also create tables by using the tools in the Tables toolbar, as shown in Exhibit 7-4, which you can view by choosing View, Toolbars, Tables. To draw a table, click the Draw Table button and drag on the page where you want to add a table. The amount you drag determines the table's size. When you release the mouse button, the Table Properties dialog box appears. In this dialog box, you can specify the number of rows and columns, as well as other formatting options.

You can use the Draw Layout Table and Draw Layout Cell tools to create custom tables in which the rows and columns might differ from each other. These tools are useful if you're using a table to control the entire layout of a page, as you can precisely control the widths and heights of each table cell. Use the Draw Layout Table tool to establish the size of the table you want, and then use the Draw Layout Cell tool to define each cell in the table.

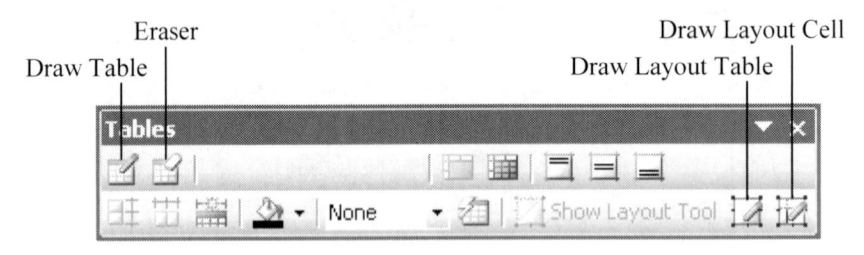

Exhibit 7-4: The Tables toolbar

Do it!

A-1: Inserting a table

Here's how	Here's why
1 Open the Outlander site	From the current unit folder.
2 Open products.htm	(From the Folder List pane.) The page contains some product images and descriptions. You'll use a table to arrange this content on the page.
3 Click to place the insertion point below the content, as shown	
4 Choose **Table**, **Insert Table…**	To open the Insert Table dialog box. There are three product descriptions, so you'll create three rows.
5 Under Size, in the Rows box, click the up arrow once	To increase the number of rows to three, in order to accommodate all three spices.
6 In the Columns box, click the up arrow once	To increase the number of columns to three. For each item, there's an image, a description, and a price.
7 Under Layout, in the Specify width box, enter **85**	To make the table span 85% of the width of the browser window. The unit of measure is set to percentage by default.
8 Click **OK**	To insert the table. You'll continue to modify this table.

Cell properties

Explanation

To use tables to arrange content, you insert the content into individual table cells. You can then format the cells as needed to create the desired arrangement. You can add content to cells by clicking a cell and typing text, by selecting text or images from other parts of the page and dragging them into a cell, or by dragging images from the Folder List pane.

You can also customize cell properties to change a table's appearance in a variety of ways. For example, you can control the alignment of content in a cell, the height and width of cells, and the space inside and between cells, and you can apply background colors and borders. To change a cell's properties, right-click the cell and choose Cell Properties. The Cell Properties dialog box opens, as shown in Exhibit 7-5.

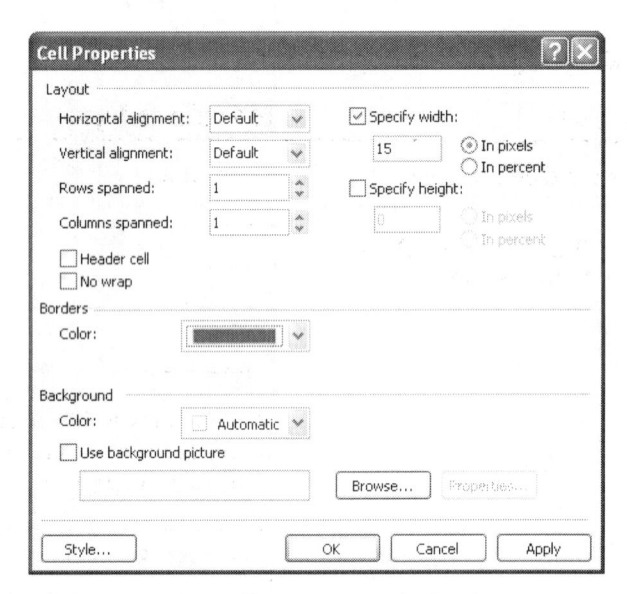

Exhibit 7-5: The Cell Properties dialog box

Cell width and height

You can set the width and height of cells by dragging their borders, or by entering values in the Specify width and Specify height boxes in the Cell Properties dialog box. When you change the width and height of one cell, the width and height of all the cells in the corresponding rows or columns adjusts to fit that cell. However, if the content in a cell requires more space than a width or height setting can accommodate, the dimensions of the cell are determined by the size of the content.

Table properties override cell properties. For example, if your table width is less than the cell width, the table width takes precedence.

The following table illustrates how table and column widths affect each other.

Column width	Table width	Resulting column width
100 pixels	500 pixels	100 pixels
100 pixels	85% (of browser)	100 pixels (if the browser width is somewhat greater than 100 pixels wide)
10% (of table)	500 pixels	50 pixels (10% of 500 pixels)
10% (of table)	85% (of browser)	8.5% of browser (10% of 85%)

Do it!

A-2: Modifying cell properties

Here's how	Here's why
1 Click the cinnamon image	To select it.
2 Drag the image into the top-left cell in the table, as shown	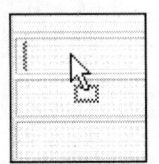 When you insert the image, the cell width increases automatically. You'll adjust the width of the cell so that it's narrower.
3 Point to the right edge of the cell	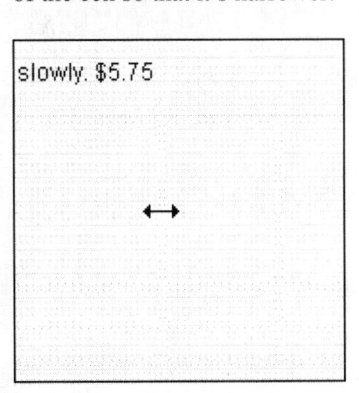 The pointer changes to a two-headed arrow, indicating that you can move the border in either direction.

4	Drag to the left, as shown	
		To decrease the width of the cell to approximately 100 pixels.
5	Select the cinnamon text, but not the price	
	Drag the text to the middle cell	
		(In the top row of the table.) Again, inserting the content increases the width of the cell.
6	Drag the right edge of the cell to the left, as shown	
		(You might need to scroll to the right to see the edge of the cell.) To decrease the width enough to make room for the price data in the right column.
7	Select and drag the cinnamon price to the top-right cell	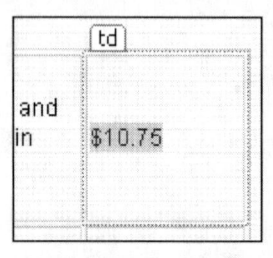
8	Add the two remaining entries to the table	Put the images in the left column cells, the descriptions in the middle cells, and the prices in the right column cells.
9	Delete the blank space above the table	Place the insertion point above the table and press Delete multiple times, as needed. Be careful not to delete any of the content within the table.

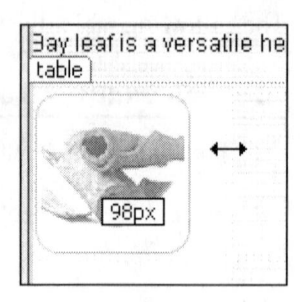

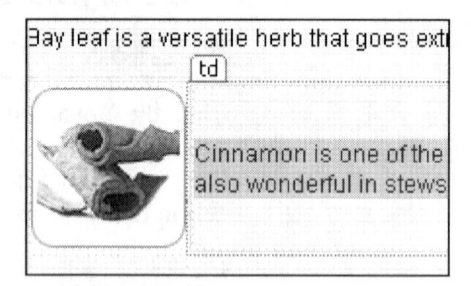

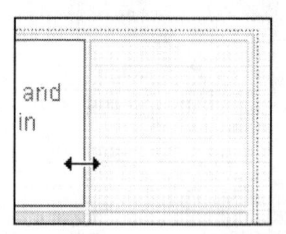

10	Save the page and preview it in Internet Explorer	The cell widths might not look exactly as they did in SharePoint Designer. For example, the right column might look wider than the left column. When you drag table cells to resize them, it can produce inconsistent results. You'll fix this.
	Close the browser	
11	Right-click in the cell containing the cinnamon image	
	Choose **Cell Properties…**	To open the Cell Properties dialog box.
12	In the Specify width box, enter **15** and select **In percent**	
	Click **OK**	You'll use the same setting for the right column.
13	Right-click the top-right cell, and choose **Cell Properties…**	To open the Cell Properties dialog box.
	Under Layout, check **Specify width**	To activate the Specify width box.
	Set a width of 15%, and click **OK**	
14	Save the page	

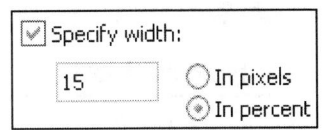

Table properties

Explanation

You can customize the formatting of a table by using the Table Properties dialog box. For example, you can change the border or background color or the amount of spacing between cells. To open the Table Properties dialog box, right-click anywhere in the table and choose Table Properties.

Table dimensions

You can drag the edge of a table to adjust its size. By default, SharePoint Designer applies height and width values in pixels. If you want to set the size of a table as a percentage of the browser window, you need to specify a percentage value in the Table Properties dialog box.

Do it!

A-3: Modifying table properties

Here's how	Here's why
1 Right-click any table cell and choose **Table Properties...**	To open the Table Properties dialog box.
2 From the Alignment list, select **Center**	*[Alignment: Center]*
	To center the table on the page.
3 In the Cell padding box, click the up arrow four times	To increase the cell padding to 5 pixels. This increases the space between the cell content and the cell borders.
In the Cell spacing box, click the down arrow twice	To remove the cell spacing. Cell spacing is the space between cells.
4 Set the table width to 90%, as shown	*[Specify width: 90, In percent]*
5 Click **OK**	To close the dialog box and apply the settings.
6 Save the page	

Inserting rows and columns

Explanation

As you work with tables, you often need to add new rows or columns. To insert a new row, click in a cell that's above or below where you want to insert a new row, and then choose Table, Insert, Row above, or Row below. If you want to add a new row to the bottom of a table, place the insertion point in the lower-right table cell and press Tab.

To insert a new column, repeat the same procedure: click in a cell to the left or right of where you want to insert a new column, and choose Table, Insert, Column to the Left, or Column to the Right.

Selecting cells, rows, and columns

You can apply formatting to multiple cells at once. For example, if you want to change the background color for all the cells in a particular row or column, select the row or column and then open the Cell Properties dialog box.

- To select multiple cells, press and hold Ctrl and click the cells you want to select.
- To select an entire row or column, point to an edge of the cell. The pointer changes to an arrow, indicating the direction of the selection when you click, as shown in Exhibit 7-6.

Exhibit 7-6: An arrow indicates the direction of the selection (either a row or column)

Do it!

A-4: Formatting rows and columns

Here's how	Here's why
1 Click anywhere in the top row	To place the insertion point. You'll add some blank space between the rows. You can do this by adding rows.
2 Choose **Table**, **Insert**, **Row Below**	To add a row between the cinnamon content and the nutmeg content.
Add a row below the nutmeg content	(Click anywhere in the nutmeg row. Then choose Table, Insert, Row Below.) Next, you'll give some of the cells a white background.
3 Point to the left edge of the first row, as shown	(The cell containing the cinnamon image.) The pointer changes to an arrow, indicating that you can select the entire row by clicking once.
Click once	To select the row.
4 Right-click the selected row and select **Cell Properties…**	To open the Cell Properties dialog box.
Under Background, from the Color list, select the white swatch	
Click **OK**	
Deselect the cell	To view the results. The table row now has a white background. You'll repeat the process for the other products in the table.
5 Select the middle row	Point to the left edge of the middle row. When the arrow appears, click once.
6 Right-click the selected row and select **Cell Properties…**	To open the Cell Properties dialog box.
From the Color list, select the white swatch	
Click **OK**	

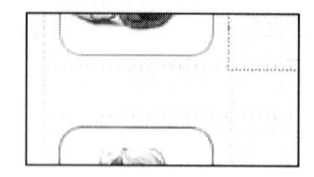

7 Give the last row a white background

8 Save the page and preview it in Internet Explorer

Close the browser

Table captions

Explanation

A table *caption* is meant to describe the content in a table. To insert a caption, place the insertion point anywhere inside the table and choose Table, Insert, Caption. A blank area appears at the top of the table. In SharePoint Designer, it looks like a table cell, but it's defined by the `<caption>` element, which is valid only within a table.

Formatting captions

By default, table captions are centered at the top of a table. You can place a caption at the bottom of a table, and you can apply other formatting options by applying a class or ID style to it. If you want to make a caption appear at the bottom of a table, right-click the caption and choose Caption Properties. In the dialog box, select Bottom of table and click OK.

Do it!

A-5: Adding a caption to a table

Here's how	Here's why
1 Right-click any table cell, and choose **Insert**, **Caption**	The table shifts down slightly and a blinking insertion point appears above the table.
Type **TOP SELLERS**	Use all capital letters. Next, you'll format the caption by using a class style.
2 In the Apply Styles pane, click **New Style**	To open the New Style dialog box.
3 In the Selector box, enter **.tableCaption**	Be sure to include a period at the beginning of the class name.
Define the style in the external style sheet globalstyles.css	
4 From the font-weight list, select **bold**	
5 From the color list, select the white swatch	
6 From the Category list, select **Background**	
From the background-color list, select **More Colors...**	To open the More Colors dialog box.
Select a dark brown color, and click **OK**	
7 Click **OK**	To close the New Style dialog box and return to the Products page.

8	Click the text **TOP SELLERS**	To place the insertion point.
	Click **<caption>**, as shown	(In the Quick Tag Selector.) To select the caption element.
9	In the Apply Styles pane, scroll down the list of styles	
	Click **.tableCaption**	To apply the style to the selection.
10	Save the page and update the style sheet	
	Preview the page in Internet Explorer	
	Close the browser	To return to SharePoint Designer.
11	Close products.htm	

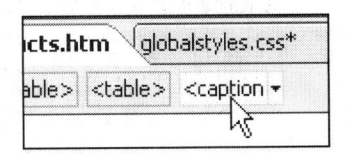

Topic B: Table-based layouts

Explanation

Even though CSS-based layouts are more efficient and easier to create and maintain, table-based layouts remain a popular design tool, because they're consistently supported by a wide variety of old and new browsers, and because the grid structure can make it easy to arrange content visually.

Nested tables

Most table-based layouts are created with nested tables. A *nested table* is simply a table that's inserted into a cell of another table. This technique often provides more flexibility for organizing and arranging information. A single table is limited to a grid of rows and columns, but nested tables allow you to create grids within grids, as illustrated in Exhibit 7-7. Table-based layouts also typically consist of merged and split cells in order to achieve a desired layout.

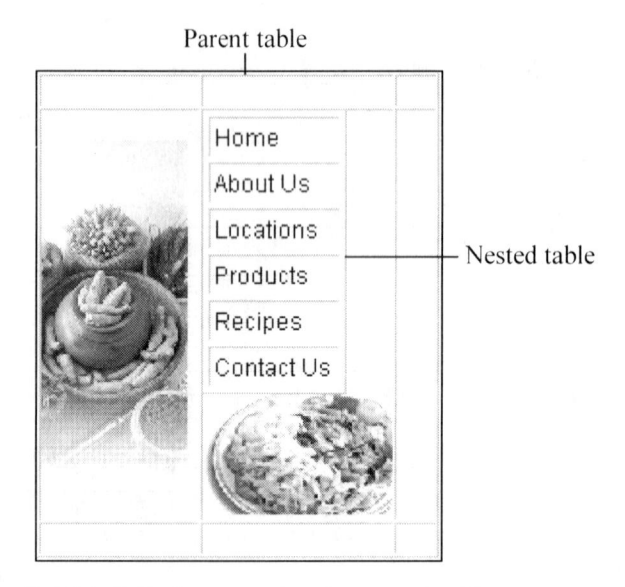

Exhibit 7-7: An example of a nested table

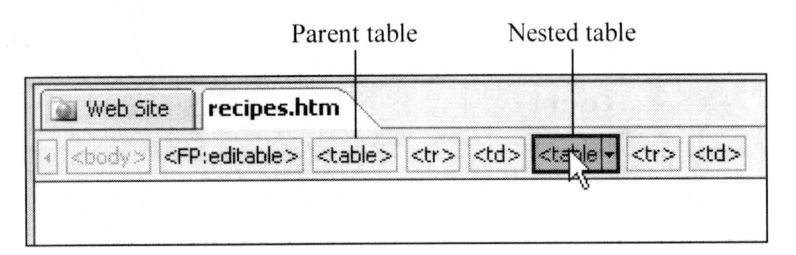

You can work with nested tables the same way you work with other tables. You just need to be sure you have the nested table selected before you adjust any table or cell formatting. To select a nested table, click one of the table cells, and click the corresponding `<table>` tag in the Quick Tag Selector, as shown in Exhibit 7-8. The Quick Tag Editor runs from left to right, so the second (or third, and so on) `<table>` tag(s) to the right always represent nested tables. When you click a `<table>` tag, the table is selected in the layout.

Exhibit 7-8: Selecting a nested table by using the Quick Tag Selector

Do it!

B-1: Updating a table-based layout

Here's how	Here's why
1 Open recipes.htm	(From the Folder List pane.) This page was added to the current site from a previous iteration of the Outlander site. The page uses a table for layout instead of CSS. You'll format the existing tables so that the page complements the rest of the pages in the site.
2 Choose **Format, Dynamic Web Template, Attach Dynamic Web Template…**	You'll link the page to the Outlander template.
Navigate to outlander.dwt, and click **Open**	The template is in the templates subfolder.
Click **Yes**	The Match Editable Regions dialog box appears.
3 Click **Content** to select the editable region and click **OK**	An alert box appears, indicating that the page has been updated.
Click **Close**	Now you'll remove the old navigation bar from the left side of the page and replace it with an image.
4 Click anywhere in the orange navigation bar	(The navigation bar runs vertically along the left side of the page.) To place the insertion point.
5 In the Quick Tag Selector, click the rightmost <table> tag	`tm*` `<table>` `<tr>` `<td>` `<table>` `<tr>` To select the nested table.
Press DELETE	To delete the content.
6 In the Folder List pane, expand the images folder	
Drag greenspices.jpg into the empty cell	The table cell automatically re-sizes to accommodate the size of the image.
Specify "Image of spices" as alternate text and click **OK**	
7 Save the page and preview it in Internet Explorer	You'll set the width of the content table so that it expands and contracts based on the size of the browser window.
Close the browser	

8	Click anywhere in the list of recipes	To place the insertion point.
9	In the Quick Tag Selector, click the rightmost <table> tag	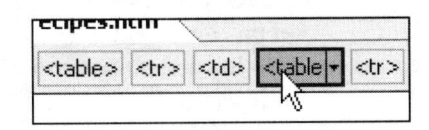 To select the nested table.
10	Right-click in the selected table	
	Choose **Table Properties…**	
	Observe the table width setting	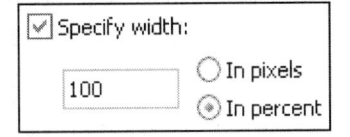 The table width is already set to 100%. However, because it's a nested table, its width depends on the width of its parent table.
	Click **Cancel**	To close the dialog box. You'll modify the width of the parent table.
11	Click the leftmost <table> tag	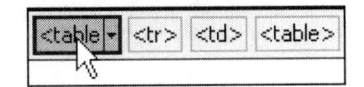 To select the parent table.
12	Right-click in the selected table	
	Choose **Table Properties…**	This table width is set to 550 pixels.
	Set the width to 85%	In the Specify width box, enter 85 and select In percent.
	Click **OK**	
13	Save the page and preview it in Internet Explorer	The content expands farther across the page, and it adjusts when the browser window is resized.
	Close the browser	
14	Close any open documents	
	Choose **File**, **Close Site**	To close the Outlander Web site.

Unit summary: Tables

Topic A In this topic, you learned how to insert tables and specify basic **formatting** options. You also learned how to modify **table properties** and **cell properties**. Then you learned how to insert and format **rows** and **columns**, and finally, you learned how to create table **captions** and apply a style to a caption.

Topic B In this topic, you learned about **table-based layouts** and **nested tables**. You learned that a nested table is a table that's inserted inside the cell of another table. Finally, you learned how to update a table-based layout.

Independent practice activity

In this activity, you'll create a new table and add content to it. Then you'll format the table cells, rows, and columns to make the content appear to be in individual rows. You'll also update an existing table-based layout. Finally, you'll update a nested table to replace a prior navigation bar with an image.

1. Open the Practice site (from the current unit folder).
2. Open **products.htm**.
3. Insert a new table before the existing page content. Give the table three rows and three columns, and a width of 85%.
4. Drag the content into the three table columns, as shown in Exhibit 7-9. Remove any excess space above or below the table.
5. Set the left and right columns so that they're each 15% of the total table width. (*Hint:* You might have to drag to widen the column containing the images, so that you can apply the cell formatting correctly.)
6. Align the table to the center of the page.
7. Add a blank table row between each product entry, as shown in Exhibit 7-10.
8. Give the rows containing the product information a white background.
9. Save the page and preview it in Internet Explorer. When you're done, close the browser to return to SharePoint Designer.
10. Open **recipes.htm**.
11. Apply the **outlander.dwt** template to the page.
12. Select the nested table used for the green navigation bar. (*Hint:* Use the Quick Tag Selector to select the nested table.)
13. Delete the table.
14. Add **orangespices.jpg** to the empty cell, as shown in Exhibit 7-11. (*Hint:* orangespices.jpg is in the images subfolder.)
15. Save and close the page. Close any other open documents.
16. Close the site.

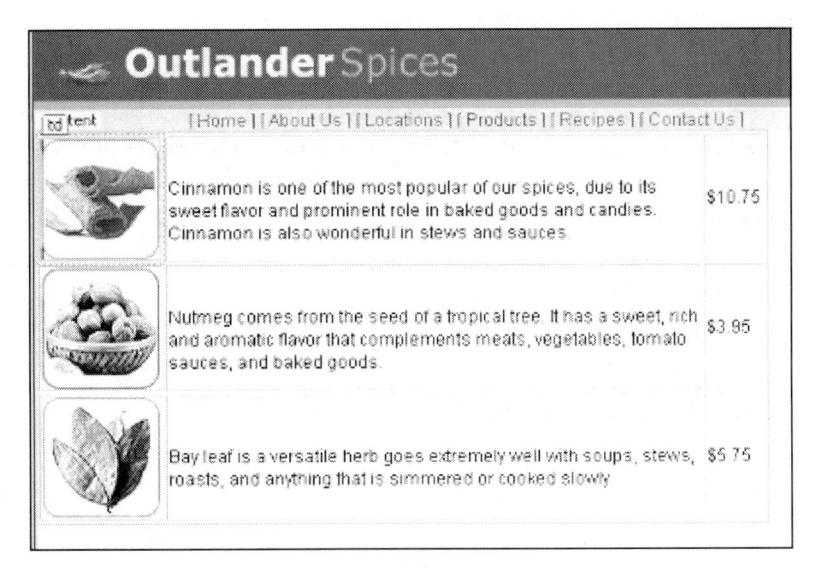

Exhibit 7-9: The Products page after step 4

Exhibit 7-10: The Products page after step 7

Exhibit 7-11: The Recipes page after step 13

Review questions

1 The width of a column is determined by:

   A the width you set for the first cell in the column.

   B the width you set for the table.

   C the width you set for an intersecting row.

   D the width of the largest cell in that column.

2 A table has a fixed width of 600 pixels. A cell inside this table has a width of 20%, and no other width is specified for another cell in its column. How many pixels wide is this column?

   A 80 pixels

   B 60 pixels

   C 160 pixels

   D 180 pixels

   E 120 pixels

3 How can you select a row in a table?

   A Triple-click one of the cells in the row you want to select.

   B Point to the row you want to select and click the arrow that appears on the left side of the row.

   C Click to place the insertion point in one of the cells in the row you want to select, and press Ctrl+A.

   D Click one of the borders between cells in the row you want to select.

4 A nested table is:

   A A table that's inserted into a row of another table.

   B A table that's inserted into a cell of another table.

   C A table with fixed dimensions.

   D A table with flexible dimensions.

5 True or false? To select a nested table, you can click to place the insertion point in the table you want to select, and click the corresponding <table> tag in the Quick Tag Selector.

Unit 8
Publishing

Unit time: 40 minutes

Complete this unit, and you'll know how to:

A Check for spelling errors throughout a site, and check for broken hyperlinks.

B Identify various options associated with publishing a site and use FTP to connect to a server.

Topic A: Proofing tools

Explanation

With SharePoint Designer, you can quickly check for spelling errors throughout the pages in your Web sites. You can also check for broken or missing hyperlinks.

Check spelling

To check for spelling errors:

1 On the Standard toolbar, click the Spelling button. The Spelling dialog box appears. You can check the entire Web site or a selected page.

2 Click Start. The dialog box expands to show a list of pages containing words that aren't in the SharePoint Designer dictionary, as shown in Exhibit 8-1. If you opt to check the entire site, the dialog box shows a list of pages where spelling errors were found.

3 For each page, you can correct spelling errors by double-clicking the page. When you do, a second spelling dialog box appears that shows you each questionable word, one at a time.

4 For each word that isn't in the SharePoint Designer dictionary, you can choose to change the spelling, ignore it, or add the word to the dictionary. When you finish checking a page, you're given the option to continue with other pages. When all words are accounted for, a message appears informing you that the spelling check is complete.

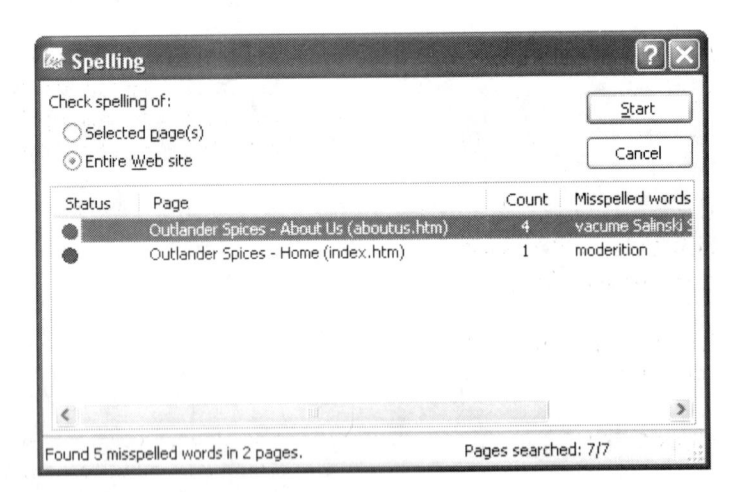

Exhibit 8-1: The Spelling dialog box

Publishing   **8–3**

Do it!   **A-1: Checking spelling**

Here's how	Here's why
1 Open the Outlander site	From the current unit folder.
2 Press F7	To open the Spelling dialog box. You can also click the Spelling button on the Standard toolbar.
3 Select **Entire Web Site** and click **Start**	SharePoint Designer searches all the documents in the Web site, and the number of spelling errors appears at the bottom of the dialog box.
4 Double-click **Outlander Spices – Home (index.htm)**	The index.htm document opens, and the Spelling dialog box changes to show spelling suggestions for the flagged entry.
5 Verify that the suggested replacement is the correct word	Not in Dictionary: moderition Change to: moderation Suggestions: moderation
Click **Change**	An alert box appears, indicating that SharePoint Designer has finished checking the page.
6 Click **Back To List**	The index.htm page closes, and the original Spelling dialog box is activated. Now the index.htm entry has a yellow circle to its left, indicating the flagged spelling has been edited.
7 Double-click **Outlander Spices – About Us (aboutus.htm)**	To open the About Us page.
8 Under Suggestions, click **vacuum**	
Click **Change**	SharePoint Designer moves to the next flagged spelling in the page, which is "Salinksi." Because this is the last name of one of the employees, you don't want to change it.
9 Click **Ignore**	Again, SharePoint Designer moves to the next flagged spelling.
Click **Ignore** through the rest of the flagged names	When you reach the end, an alert box appears, indicating that SharePoint Designer has finished checking all pages.
10 Click **Back To List**	To close the About Us page and return to the original Spelling dialog box.
11 Click **Cancel**	To close the Spelling dialog box.

Check hyperlinks

Explanation

As you prepare to upload a Web site, it's a good idea to check for any broken hyperlinks. Previewing the site and clicking every link would be a tedious task. Fortunately, SharePoint Designer can check the integrity of local and external links for you.

To check hyperlinks throughout a site, choose Task Panes, Hyperlinks to open the Hyperlinks pane, as shown in Exhibit 8-2. When you open this pane, SharePoint Designer automatically searches the site and displays a list of any broken hyperlinks.

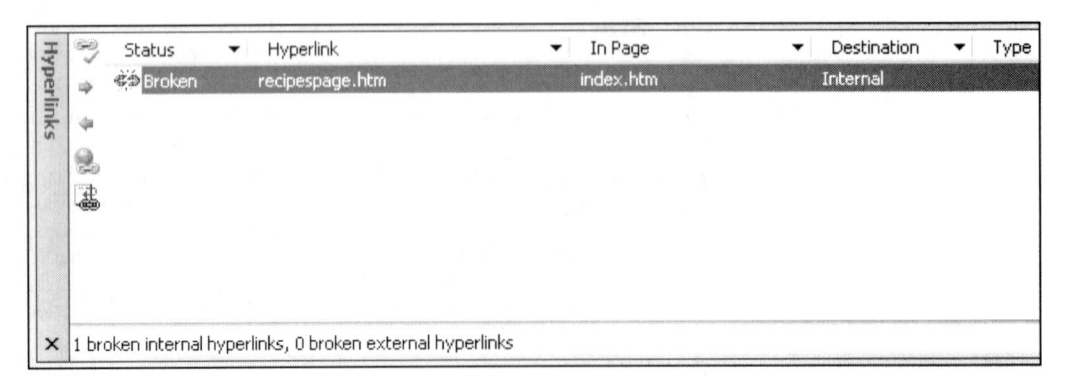

Exhibit 8-2: The Hyperlinks pane

To fix a hyperlink, double-click the page name or select it and click the Edit Hyperlink button on the left side. When you do, the Edit Hyperlink dialog box appears, as shown in Exhibit 8-3. In this dialog box, you can update the hyperlink with the correct target file or URL. Sometimes, you might want to see the location of the hyperlink in the page to correct the problem. You can open the page where the hyperlink resides by clicking the Edit Page button. You can also open the page beforehand by double-clicking it in the Hyperlinks pane.

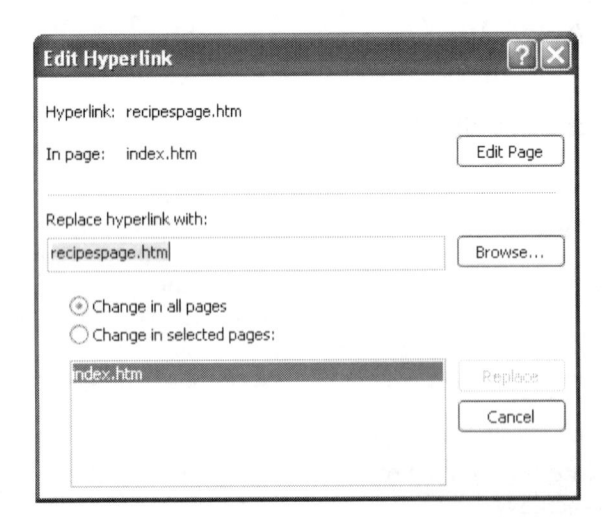

Exhibit 8-3: The Edit Hyperlink dialog box

Do it!

A-2: Checking hyperlinks

Here's how	Here's why
1 Choose **Task Panes**, **Hyperlinks**	The Hyperlinks pane appears below the Web Site list in the center of the workspace. One broken hyperlink is listed for the index.htm document.
2 Double-click **recipespage.htm**	To open the Edit Hyperlink dialog box. Instead of recipespage.htm, the hyperlink should be recipes.htm.
3 Click **Browse...**	The Edit Hyperlink dialog box shows a list of all the files in the site.
In the list, select **recipes.htm** and click **OK**	You'll fix the link throughout the site, in case there are other places where the incorrect document title is used.
4 Verify that **Change in all pages** is selected, and click **Replace**	The dialog box closes and the Hyperlinks pane is empty.
5 Close the Hyperlinks pane	

Topic B: Web site publishing

Explanation

When you're finished building your Web site, you need to publish it on the Internet so that users can access it. *Publishing* a Web site simply means copying your Web site to a Web server.

Publishing on the Web

To publish a Web site, you need an Internet Service Provider (ISP). ISPs provide you with a domain name and a server. A *domain name* is the name that identifies your Web site on the Internet. For example, www.outlanderspices.com is a domain name that identifies the Outlander Spices Web site. You publish your pages to a Web server, which handles permissions, executes programs, and communicates with client computers that make requests to the server.

Network publishing

To share your Web site with others in your organization, you can publish it on a local network, also known as a local area network (LAN). A *LAN* is a group of computers and related equipment that are spread over a small area (usually within a building or a few adjacent buildings) and connected to share resources and information. This type of Web site is often referred to as an *intranet* site.

To publish your Web site on the local network, you need to install Internet Information Server (IIS). After installing IIS, you can publish your Web site on the Web server on your machine.

After you publish a Web site on a local network, anyone connected to the network can access your Web site by typing the network ID of your machine in the Address bar of a browser. You can also set permissions and properties for your Web sites to determine access limits for different users.

You can also use IIS as a platform to test how your Web site appears and functions, before actually publishing it to the Web. Then, you can publish the Web site from your local server to the server provided by your ISP.

IIS also supports complex interactive technologies, such as Common Gateway Interface (CGI) and Active Server Pages (ASP).

Publishing Web sites to multiple locations

You can publish Web sites to various locations, such as local-to-remote, remote-to-local, or remote-to-remote servers. For example, you might want to publish a Web site that you've created to the local intranet, as well as to a Web server on the Internet. You can also publish a Web site to a location on your local computer.

You can publish your SharePoint Designer Web sites on the Internet to an HTTP server, Web server, or an FTP server. To publish to an HTTP server, your ISP should have the Microsoft SharePoint Designer Server Extensions or SharePoint team services installed. You can also publish your Web site to the SharePoint Portal Server, if it's installed on your machine or if you're connected to it.

After you've published a Web site, you can publish the same Web site to other locations. To do this, follow the same steps and specify the new destinations or server names.

Do it!

B-1: Discussing Web servers

Questions and answers

1 You've created a Web site. Before publishing it on the Internet, you want to verify that the Web site is working properly. What can you do?

2 Can you publish a Web site to the Internet after you've published it to a local network?

3 How can you make your local computer act as a Web server?

4 After you publish a SharePoint Designer Web site to your local computer, you want to publish it to an HTTP server provided by your ISP. What do you need to do this?

Remote Web Site view

Explanation

You can use the options in the Remote Web Site view to publish a site by using any of the following protocols:

- **SharePoint Designer or SharePoint Services:** A Remote Web server that supports SharePoint Designer Server Extensions or SharePoint Services.
- **WebDAV:** A Remote Web server that supports Distributed Authoring and Versioning (DAV).
- **FTP:** A remote Web server that supports File Transfer Protocol.
- **File System:** An option that uses a folder on your local computer or on the network as the Remote Web Site.

To publish a Web site, you first need to establish the server type you want to use. With the site open, click Remote Web Site in the Views bar. If you haven't applied any remote settings for the site yet, the window is empty. Near the top-right corner, click Remote Web Site Properties to open the Remote Web Site Properties dialog box, as shown in Exhibit 8-4. You can then select any of the four server types. In the Remote Web site location box, enter the location where you want to publish the Web site or click Browse to find the location. The location could be your machine name or the server name provided by your ISP.

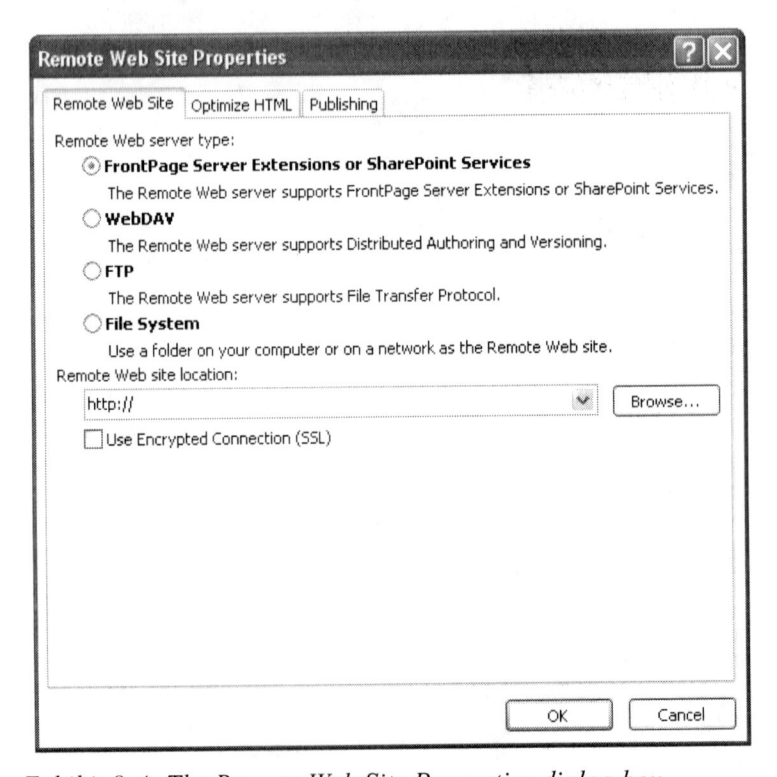

Exhibit 8-4: The Remote Web Site Properties dialog box

When you've entered the desired settings, click OK. If you've established settings for a remote location, a small dialog box appears asking you for your user name and password. If the site is to be an intranet site, the site administrator typically assigns the user name and password. If the site is to be an Internet site, the ISP administers the user name and password. The ISP should allow you to create a user name and password of your choice. After you've entered the correct information, click OK. The Remote Web Site view window shows two panes, similar to the example in Exhibit 8-5. The left pane shows the current site folder, and the right pane shows the files, if any, stored at the remote site location. To upload the site, click Publish Web site.

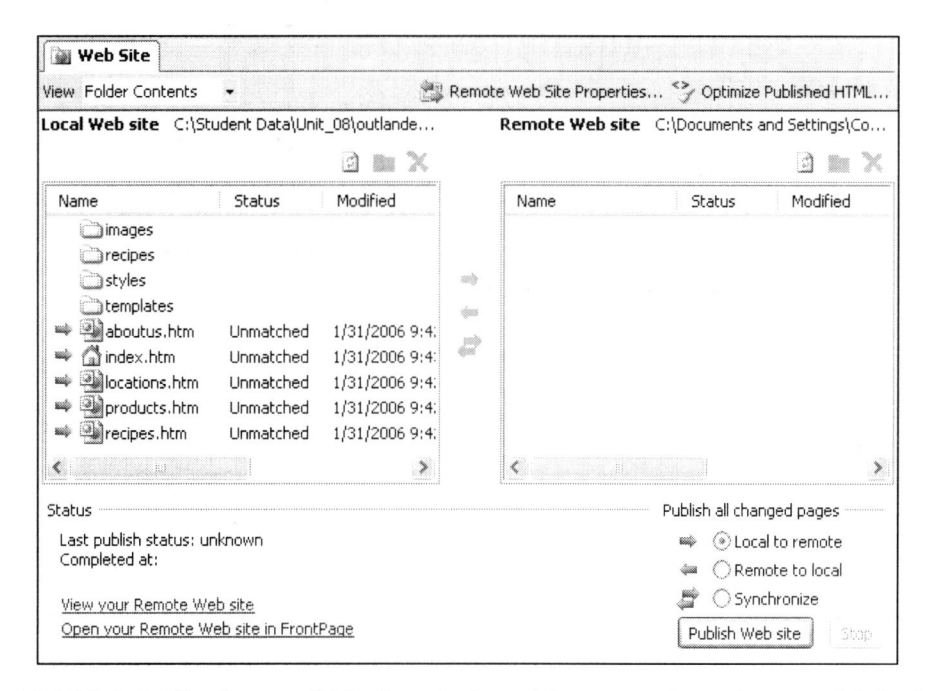

Exhibit 8-5: The Remote Web Site window with remote site options established

Setting publishing options

When you publish a Web site to a server, you can set various publishing options by activating the Publishing tab in the Remote Web Site Properties dialog box, as shown in Exhibit 8-6. You can set options to publish only those pages that have changed since you last published the Web site, or to publish all pages by overwriting the ones that already exist at the destination.

You can also set options to determine the changes that have been made since you last published the Web site, either by comparing the source and destination Web sites, or by using time stamps on the source files. It's also possible to set options to log changes during publishing. You can later view these log files to see the changes. *Log files* contain information about the changes made in the Web site, such as who made the changes, when they took place, and which pages were modified.

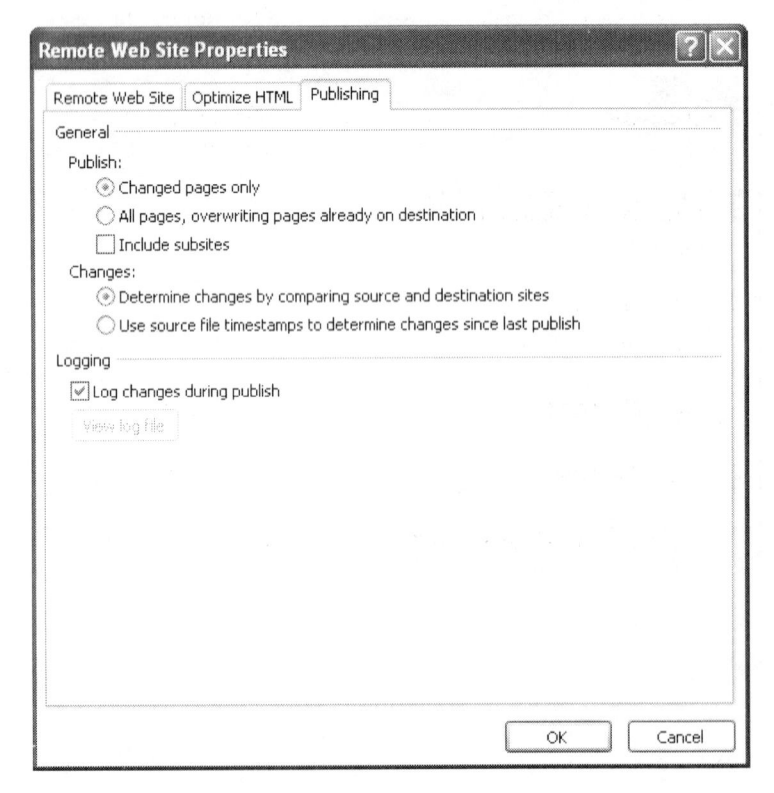

Exhibit 8-6: Publishing options

Do it!

B-2: Connecting to a server by using secure FTP

Here's how	Here's why
1 In the Views bar, click **Remote Web Site**	
2 At the top of the window, click **Remote Web Site Properties...**	To open the Remote Web Site Properties dialog box.
3 Select **FTP**	
4 Edit the Remote Web site location box to read **ftp://outlanderspices.com**	To specify the address of an FTP host where files will be sent.
Click **OK**	The Name and Password Required dialog box appears.
5 In the Name box, enter your first name	
6 In the Password box, enter **password**	
7 Click **Cancel**	To close the dialog box.
8 Click **Cancel**	To close the dialog box.
9 Choose **File**, **Close Site**	To close the Outlander Web site.

SharePoint Portal Server

Explanation

You can use Microsoft SharePoint Portal Server to create Web portals. *Web portals* are Web sites that offer various services, such as e-mail, search engines, online shopping, and forums. You can establish a central point of access to all your key business information and applications by using SharePoint Portal Server. You can also share information across file servers, databases, public folders, Internet sites, and SharePoint Team Services-based Web sites.

If your local computer has the SharePoint Portal Server installed, then the Web sites that you publish to your local computer act as functional Web sites. The *SharePoint Portal Server* is a set of programs that extend the functionality of a Web server to your local computer. It's possible to publish your Web site from your local computer to the SharePoint Portal Server, even if your computer doesn't have SharePoint Portal Server. You can do this by connecting your machine to one with SharePoint Portal Server installed.

To publish a Web site to the SharePoint Portal Server:

1. Chose File, Publish Site to open the Remote Web Site Properties dialog box.
2. Under Remote Web server type, select SharePoint Designer or SharePoint Services.
3. In the Remote Web site location box, enter the address of the SharePoint Portal Server and click OK.
4. When the Web site opens in Remote Web site view, click Publish Web site.

Do it!

B-3: Discussing SharePoint Portal Server

Questions and answers

1. What is a SharePoint Portal Server?

2. What's the procedure to publish a Web site to the SharePoint Portal Server?

3. If your local computer doesn't have SharePoint Portal Server, can you publish your Web site from your local computer to the SharePoint Portal Server?

Unit summary: Publishing

Topic A In this topic, you learned how to check for spelling errors throughout all pages in a Web site. You also fixed **broken hyperlinks** in a site by using the Hyperlinks pane.

Topic B In this topic, you learned about various options associated with **publishing** a site, and you established the settings necessary to upload a site by using **FTP**. You also learned about **Microsoft SharePoint Portal Server** and how you can use it to improve the functionality of a Web site.

Independent practice activity

In this activity, you'll check a completed Web site for spelling errors and broken links. You'll also establish settings for publishing the site using FTP.

1 Open the Practice site (from the current unit folder).

2 Check for spelling errors throughout the entire site. Skip employee names, if they're flagged.

3 Check for any broken hyperlinks in the site. If any broken links are found, correct them. Close the Hyperlinks pane when you're finished.

4 Close any open documents, if necessary, and then switch to the Remote Web Site view.

5 Open the Remote Web Site Properties dialog box.

6 Enter settings appropriate for publishing a site using FTP. Use ftp://outlanderspices.com as the remote location.

7 Click Cancel to cancel the settings.

8 Close the site.

9 Close SharePoint Designer.

Review questions

1 True or false? To check for spelling errors throughout all the pages in a site, you must open each page individually.

2 When checking for broken hyperlinks in the Hyperlinks pane, how can you open a page in which a broken hyperlink exists. (Choose all that apply.)

  A Select the page listed in the task pane and choose File, Open.

  B Double-click the page listed in the task pane.

  C Select the page listed in the task pane and choose View, Page.

  D Click the Edit Hyperlink button and click Edit Page.

3 True or false? The text *www.outlanderspices.com* is an example of a domain name that identifies a site on the Web.

4 Which of the following are server types available using SharePoint Designer? (Choose all that apply.)

  A WebDAV

  B DWT services

  C FTP

  D SharePoint Services

5 When you publish a Web site to a server, you can set various publishing options by activating the:

  A Upload tab in the Remote Web Site Properties dialog box.

  B Publishing tab in the Publish Site dialog box.

  C Publishing tab in the Remote Web Site Properties dialog box.

  D Publishing tab in the SharePoint Services Settings dialog box.

Course summary

This summary contains information to help you bring the course to a successful conclusion. Using this information, you'll be able to:

A Use the summary text to reinforce what you've learned in class.

B Determine the next courses in this series, if any, as well as any other resources that might help you continue to learn about SharePoint Designer 2007.

Topic A: Course summary

Use the following summary text to reinforce what you've learned in class.

Unit summaries

Unit 1

In this unit, you learned the basics of the **Internet**, **Web**, and **HTML**. You identified the main components of the **SharePoint Designer interface**, and you learned how to **customize the workspace**. Then you performed basic **Web page editing** by adding and formatting text and images, and you **previewed a page in Internet Explorer**. Lastly, you learned about **HTML tags** and how to **select page elements**.

Unit 2

In this unit, you learned the basics of **site planning**. You learned how to **create a one-page Web site** and add folders and pages to it, and finally, you created and edited a **template**, and applied a template to existing pages.

Unit 3

In this unit, you **imported content** from an external document. Then you **converted line breaks to paragraphs**, inserted **spaces** and **symbols**, and created **headings** and **lists**. Finally, you learned how to create an **external style sheet** and establish **element** and **class styles**.

Unit 4

In this unit, you learned how to **define content sections** with the <div> element; create and apply **ID styles**; apply **margins**, **padding**, and **borders** to an element; and create and modify a **two-column layout**.

Unit 5

In this unit, you learned about different **image file formats**, and you set basic **image properties** and applied **alternate text**. Finally, you learned how to **arrange images** relative to adjacent content.

Unit 6

In this unit, you created **links**, **link bars**, **e-mail links**, and **bookmarks**. You also customized **link styles**, created an image map, and **linked hotspots** to bookmarks.

Unit 7

In this unit, you created and formatted a **table** and individual **cells**, inserted and formatted **rows** and **columns**, and created and formatted a table **caption**. Finally, you learned how to work with **nested tables** in a table-based layout.

Unit 8

In this unit, you **checked for spelling errors** and **broken hyperlinks** throughout a Web site, **identified various options** associated with **publishing a site**, and **connected to a server by using FTP**.

Topic B: Continued learning after class

It's impossible to learn to use any software effectively in a single day. To get the most out of this class, you should begin working with Microsoft SharePoint Designer 2007 to perform real tasks as soon as possible. Course Technology also offers resources for continued learning.

Next courses in this series

This is the first course in this series. The next course in this series is:

- *SharePoint Designer 2007: Advanced*
    - Work with multimedia files
    - Apply behaviors and rollovers
    - Create layers and dynamic layers
    - Create and format layout tables
    - Create forms and apply field validation
    - Apply an XML data source to a Web page
    - Apply basic search engine optimization
    - Check a site for problems before publishing

Other resources

You might find some of these other resources useful as you continue to learn about Microsoft SharePoint Designer 2007. For more information, visit www.course.com.

- *HTML 4.0: Basic*
  ISBN: 1-4188-3806-3

- *HTML 4.0: Advanced*
  ISBN: 0-619-20262-9

- *XHTML: Authoring and Design Techniques*
  ISBN: 0-619-20265-3

SharePoint Designer 2007: Basic

Quick reference

Button	Shortcut keys	Function
	CTRL + N	Creates a new blank page
	CTRL + O	Opens a Web page or file
		Shows or hides formatting marks
	CTRL + S	Saves a Web page, template, or style sheet
	F12	Previews the Web page in a browser
		Formats the selected text as a bulleted list
		Formats the selected text as a numbered list
		Increases the indentation of the selected paragraph or text to the next tab stop
	F7	Checks a Web site for spelling errors
	CTRL + K	Inserts a hyperlink for the selected text
		Inserts an image in a Web page
		Creates a rectangular hotspot
		Creates a polygonal hotspot
		Draws a table in the Web page

Glossary

Bookmarks
Targets on a page that you can link to. Bookmarks work well with pages that have a lot of content.

Class styles
Named styles that can be used as many times as needed per page.

Definition list
An HTML list for structuring terms and their corresponding definitions, for use in glossaries, frequently asked question (FAQ) pages, or similar contexts.

Element styles
Define the formatting of HTML elements. An element style overrides any default formatting for an HTML element.

External links
Links to a page or resource outside your Web site.

External style sheet
An external text file that's saved with a .css extension and contains style rules that determine how HTML elements are displayed.

Font set
A set of three or more similar font faces that help ensure consistent text display in a variety of browsers and operating systems.

GIF
An image format that can contain a maximum of 256 colors, so it's best suited for images that have relatively few colors and areas of flat color, such as line drawings, logos, and image-based text.

Home page
The top-level page in a Web site. It's usually named index.htm or default.htm.

HTML
Hypertext Markup Language, a standard markup language on the Web. HTML consists of *tags* that define the basic structure of a Web page.

Hyperlink
Text or an image that, when clicked, connects the user to another page or Web site.

ID styles
Named styles that may be applied to only one element per page.

Image map
An image that contains multiple links called hotspots.

Internal style sheet
One or more style rules embedded in the head section of a document. Styles in an internal style sheet can influence elements only in that single document.

Internet
A vast array of electronic networks that belong to universities, businesses, organizations, governments, and individuals all over the world.

JPEG
An image format that supports more than 16 million colors, so it's best suited for photographs and images that have many subtle color shadings.

Link states
The four conditions of a link; link, hover, active, and visited.

Local links
Links to pages or resources within your Web site.

Margin
The space between a page's content and the edge of the browser window, or the space between individual elements.

Nested list
A list inside another list.

Nested table
A table that's inserted in the cell of another table.

Non-breaking space
A special HTML character that inserts a single space without breaking a line.

Ordered list
An HTML list structure that automatically appends sequential labels to each list item. By default, list items are numbered 1, 2, 3, and so on.

PNG
An image format that combines some of the best features of JPEG and GIF, supporting more than 16 million colors and many levels of transparency. Many older browsers don't support the PNG format.

Sans-serif fonts
Fonts whose characters do not have the flourishes that serif fonts have.

Serif fonts
Fonts whose characters have designs called "flourishes" at the tips of their letters.

Table cell
The intersection of a row and column in a table. You insert content into table cells.

Uniform Resource Locator (URL)
A unique address used by browsers to locate Web pages and the servers they reside on.

Unordered list
An HTML list structure that automatically appends bullets to each list item.

Web
One of many services of the Internet. Other Internet services include e-mail, File Transfer Protocol (FTP), and instant messaging.

Web site
A collection of linked pages displayed on the World Wide Web.

Index

A

Alternate text, 5-6

B

Background images, 2-16, 2-17
Bookmarks, 6-10
Breaks, 3-4

C

Cascading Style Sheets (CSS), 3-8, 3-16
CSS
 Layout, 4-2

D

Documents
 Headings, 3-11

E

Element styles, 3-22

G

GIF image format, 5-2

H

Home pages, 1-2, 2-5
Hotspots, 6-18
HTML
 Class styles, 3-26
 Element styles, 3-22
 Elements, 1-20
 Tags, 1-20
HTML elements
 <div> tags, 4-2
 Block elements, 4-11
 Borders, 4-14
 Floating, 4-18, 4-21
 ID styles, 4-5, 4-8
 Inline elements, 4-11
 Margins, 4-14
 Padding, 4-14
Hyperlinks, 1-2, 6-2
 Checking, 8-4
Hypertext Markup Language (HTML), 1-2

I

Image formats, 5-2
Image maps, 6-18
Image-based text, 5-8
Images
 Alternate text, 5-6
 Borders, 5-14
 File formats, 5-2
 GIFs, 5-2
 JPEGs, 5-2
 Layout, 5-10
 Margins, 5-12
 Padding, 5-14
 PNGs, 5-2
 Properties, 5-3
 Sources, 5-2
Importing content, 3-2
IntelliSense, 1-21
Interface, 1-4
Internet, 1-2
Internet services, 1-2
Intranet sites, 8-6

J

JPEG image format, 5-2

L

Layouts
 Nested tables, 7-16
 Table-based, 7-16
Line breaks, 3-4
Link bars, 6-4
Links, 6-2
 External, 6-7
 Local, 6-2
 States, 6-14
 Styles, 6-14
 Visited, 6-14
Lists, 3-13
 Definition, 3-14
 Nested, 3-14
 Ordered, 3-13
Local Area Networks (LANs), 8-6
Local links, 6-2

M

Margins, 2-15

N

Navigation bar, 4-2
Navigation bars, 6-4
Non-breaking spaces, 3-6

P

Padding, 5-14
Paragraph breaks, 3-4
PNG image format, 5-2
Publishing, 8-6
   Log files, 8-10

Q

Quick Tag Selector, 1-23

S

Site plans
   Basic elements, 2-2
Spelling
   Checking, 8-2
Style sheets
   External, 3-19
   Internal, 3-16
Symbols, 3-7

T

Tables
   Captions, 7-14
   Cell properties, 7-6
   Creating, 7-2
   Inserting, 7-3
   Inserting rows and columns, 7-11
   Nested, 7-16
   Properties, 7-10
Task panes, 1-5
   Arranging, 1-7
Templates, 2-10
   Applying, 2-18
   Editable regions, 2-12
   Style sheets, 3-19
Text
   Importing, 3-2
Tiling background images, 2-16, 2-17

U

Uniform Resource Locaters (URLs), 1-2

V

Views, 1-10

W

Web page
   Layouts, 4-10
   Previewing, 1-18
Web pages
   Content, 1-14
   Editing, 1-12
   Elements, 1-13
   Margins, 2-15
   Properties, 2-15
Web portals, 8-12
Web sites
   Adding pages, 2-7
   Design elements, 2-2
   Local, 2-5
   Moving documents, 2-7
   Planning, 2-2
   Structure, 2-4
World Wide Web, 1-2